KING PE...

Celebration of ...

Eric Rolls was born in 1925, and brought up in northern New South Wales. Since 1948 he has farmed his own land, first at Boggabri, then at Baradine.

His published work includes collections of poetry and children's books. He spent six years researching and writing *A Million Wild Acres,* for which he was awarded the *Age* Australian Book of the Year in 1981.

He is currently working on a history of the Chinese in Australia.

BY THE SAME AUTHOR:

VERSE
Sheaf Tosser (1967)
The Green Mosaic: Memories of New Guinea
(1977)

GENERAL
They all Ran Wild (1969)
The River (1974)
A Million Wild Acres (1981)

FOR CHILDREN
Running Wild (1973)
Miss Strawberry (1978)

Eric Rolls
Celebration of the Senses

A KING PENGUIN
PUBLISHED BY PENGUIN BOOKS

Penguin Books Australia Ltd,
487 Maroondah Highway, P.O. Box 257
Ringwood, Victoria, 3134, Australia
Penguin Books Ltd,
Harmondsworth, Middlesex, England
40 West 23rd Street, New York, N.Y. 10010. U.S.A.
Penguin Books Canada Ltd,
2801 John Street, Markham, Ontario, Canada L3R 1B4
Penguin Books (N.Z.) Ltd,
182-190 Wairau Road, Auckland 10, New Zealand

First published 1984 by Thomas Nelson Australia
Published in Penguin, 1985

Copyright © Eric Rolls, 1984

All Rights Reserved. Without limiting the rights under copyright reserved above, no part of this publication may be reproduced, stored in or introduced into a retrieval system, or transmitted, in any form or by any means (electronic, mechanical, photocopying, recording or otherwise), without the prior written permission of both the copyright owner and the above publisher of this book.

Offset from the Thomas Nelson Australia edition
Made and printed in Australia by
The Dominion Press–Hedges & Bell, Victoria

CIP

Rolls, Eric C. (Eric Charles), 1923-
Celebration of the senses.

ISBN 0 14 008508 4.

I. Title.

A828'.308

Contents

Sight 1

Taste 41

Hearing 76

Touch and Feelings 102

Smell 144

Free Choice 156

for Joan

Sight

I came in again to see if she was awake. The old blue sheet that covered her had torn during the night. Her left buttock shone through the split like an early morning moon.

This book has no form. One cannot order the senses. They surprise constantly if one keeps aware. Accept their messages, judge them with the imagination, then celebrate.

Meet Joan earlier at a time of crisis. That is a good time to meet people – their qualities are exposed. She got out of bed suddenly in the early hours of the morning. 'Something popped inside me' she said. 'It must be coming.' She switched on the light, lifted her flimsy nightie and comically tried to peer over her swollen belly at her vulva dripping on to the polished pine floor. 'The bag must have burst early. Look at the mess I'm making. Would you get me a towel to stand on?' She shook one wet foot, then the other.

'Any pains yet?'

'Not much. Do you think I ought to go in now? I don't want to be waiting there for hours.'

'I'll ring the hospital' I said. 'And we better go now. The road is doubtful.'

'Put another towel on the car seat. I'll just pull on a coat. There's no sense in getting dressed.'

We were staying with my parents. It was a wet year and our own farm was isolated by a flooded river and a banked-up creek. The road to town then was thirty kilometres of gravel and five of bitumen. I had to concentrate on driving. The gravel was greasy in parts. We spoke little. She assessed her pains.

'They're coming regularly now.'

'Are they bad?'

'Nothing I can't bear.'

The worst of the road was a three-kilometre side-track

Celebration

skirting a stretch of deep loose soil piled on an intended extension of the bitumen. The manoeuvrable little Peugeot began to swing. I had to change down to second. The car swung like a pendulum. I applied power slowly when it faced the right way, eased off and corrected when it swung. The front slid, the back slid. Power at the wrong time would twist the car all the way round, correction too late would allow it to slide off the track and bog. We got through.

At the hospital I told the sister 'I don't think she'll be long now. The pains are coming fairly often.'

'It's her first, isn't it?' said the sister unconcernedly. 'She'll be hours yet.' She took her by the arm and led her away before I had kissed her, before I had even wished her well. In 1955 husbands at a birth were unthought of. I drove back to bed. But even before I had undressed the hospital rang to say we had a son. I drove in again.

Her appearance astonished me. She looked uncharacteristically coarse. Her eyes were big and tired, her cheeks slack, her mouth loose. I kissed her.

'I saw him born. They wanted to give me gas but I pushed it away. The doctor cut me a little. I didn't want that. "You'll tear" he said "and a tear is harder to sew up and takes longer to heal." So I let him cut me. I didn't think I'd need cutting.' She looked disappointed.

'It won't disfigure you and it's not an aberration.' One never knows if words comfort. Doubts are generally insoluble in words. They persist like lumps in sauce.

'He came so fast. The sister wouldn't believe I'd not be long. She left me on my own and there wasn't any bell. I tried to get out of bed to call someone and I was sick all over the bed. Someone in the corridor heard me and called the nurse. She was nearly too late to shave me. She was rough and cross. "What a mess! Where's your basin?" she said. I told her there wasn't one. "I'll have to clean you up later. There's hardly time to shave you. You should have been done hours ago. Keep still." I was afraid she'd cut me. The bed smelt awful.'

Now I understood her appearance. All female mammals after giving birth have that same unmoulded look. For an hour, for hours, their bodies take them over. All they can do is yield. They lose their will.

Sight

'I've fed him' she said. 'He sucked strongly. It was a wonderful feeling. They won't leave him with me. I'll ring for the nurse to bring him in.' She proudly showed me a perfect baby. 'I'll bring him home as soon as I can. I want him with me.'

That was Kim, our first son. Kerry Jane, our daughter, was born in Newcastle at a more modern hospital. She stayed in the room with her mother and it was a happy experience. Babies there were treated as interesting guests who had newly arrived, not appendices who had been amputated.

When Mitchell, our third child, was born, we set off for the hospital just after daylight. The lamb I had killed the evening before was hanging in its calico shroud beneath the killing tree.

'Wait and cut the lamb up first' said Joan. 'It might get too hot.'

She had a sudden, sharper pain. 'The lamb can wait' I said. 'You can't.'

We did not know it was an occasional joke of the young nurses to rush in and say 'Quick! There's a woman having a baby on the steps of the hospital.' The nurse who did rush in was not taken seriously. It was two or three minutes before anyone came. I helped her towards the delivery-room door and there was dismissed. I abandoned her to the care of the nurses and the doctor who had not yet been called. The nurses seemed incapable of helping her on to the high delivery table. With our second son's head about to protrude between her legs she hauled herself up. Now, too late, I would carry her in against any opposition.

We did not take our children too earnestly. They were an accident of our lovemaking, even if inevitable and welcome. They fitted into our lives; they did not take us over. We had no patience with those who spoke of their responsibilities to their children as though children made living a duty. Our responsibility was to love life. And our children joined us.

Country children grow up fitting sex and birth into life as naturally as it ought to fit. Still, I was astonished to learn when our children were all under seven that they had named the Dorset Horn rams according to their sexual capacities. There were Greedy, Clumsy, Shy, Big Balls, Weary Slowcoach, Jealous – several more. The children

Celebration

saw the sheep often. Sheep need a lot of attention when run under intensive conditions, especially at lambing, and the children usually rode round the ewes as soon as they got home from school. Their small hands were expert at delivering lambs. They could reach in easily to straighten a bent foreleg. A serious mal-presentation such as a turned-back head was beyond them. It needs strength to push the lamb back in to where there is room to pull its head forward. The ewe bleats her agony and pushes with all her force against the reversal.

I once lambed nearly four hundred ewes when they themselves were still technically lambs. A sheep becomes a hogget with two permanent teeth on the bottom jaw at about fourteen months. These big crossbred ewes were eleven to twelve months old. The season was lush and although I had tried to limit their feeding they had had too much to eat during the last three months of pregnancy. Their lambs grew too big for them to bear, even the twins and triplets. During the two to three weeks it took them all to lamb, I spent most of every day with them from daylight to dark. So many needed help I did not wait for them to exhaust themselves with twelve hours or more of straining so that I could catch them easily. I drove around the flock in the car, a shepherd's crook beside me, an intelligent and well-trained Kelpie named Raff in the open boot. The sheep were accustomed to the car and took little notice of it. When we came to a ewe with the nose and forelegs of a lamb bulging from her vulva, I stopped the car and Raff hopped quietly out of the boot. He knew as well as I did which ewe had to be caught. Without any orders he singled her out, chased her and brought her at the run past me. I held out the shepherd's crook and caught her by the neck. Raff hopped into the boot again, out of sight so that he did not disturb any more ewes than was necessary; I strode the ewe and rode her into one of the portable pens I had erected all about the paddock. There I would pull the lamb away and leave the ewe to lick it and fuss over it till it got to its feet and sucked. If I had not penned her she would have bolted in fright after being disturbed by the dog and forgotten the lamb she had not smelt.

Often on the first inspection each morning I would find

Sight

an abandoned lamb or two wandering aimlessly and bleating, or else collapsed in a sad heap in the grass. They were usually the last-born of triplets. Their brothers or sisters, sturdier by fifteen or twenty minutes, had given them no opportunity at the udder. I would pick the lamb up and give it to the last ewe that had been penned. She would still have colostrum available, that thick yellow first milk streaked with blood essential for its laxative and protective qualities. Ewes recognise their lambs first by smell. It is only after several days they know them by voice as well. So to make the strange lamb acceptable I would smear it with any birth slime still in the pen and drape it with any scraps of afterbirth the ewe had not eaten. A few drops of vanilla on the back of the lamb and a dab on the ewe's nose served just as well.

One ewe refused the lamb I pulled from her. She butted it savagely against the panels of her yard. So we gave her a tranquilliser three times a day. She grew amiable, smelt her lamb, bleated to it, fed it. After a week we stopped her pills. She butted the lamb so hard she knocked it through the steel panels and right out of the yard. I marked her as an incorrigible mother with a red tag in her ear – she would go with the next draft of sheep to slaughter – and gave the week-old lamb to a ewe of easy temperament.

A big Friesian heifer began to calve late one afternoon. She was the right age, the right size. I expected her to have an easy birth. The next morning I found her huge calf dead. It weighed sixty kilogrammes. The heifer lay in front of it with sad and frightened eyes. She had strained so hard she broke her back.

A girl dressed in yellow, a superb dancer, made a bitter commentary on birth on a Melbourne stage. She moved lightly and easily at first, stiffening occasionally in spasms that became more frequent. She danced on to a bed and began to tumble over and over, backwards and forwards. The speed of her movement increased till she was a whirling mass of yellow. She went on till the audience fidgeted. They feared for her. She stopped suddenly, exhausted and dazed. And produced from between her legs a dead mullet.

Traditional Greek women prefer to have their babies standing up. They grasp the foot of the bed, spread their

Celebration

legs and shriek. Their attendants – mother, grandmother, friend, village midwife – stretch their hands blindly beneath the long black skirt and catch the baby as it comes. This method is frowned on in modern Australian maternity hospitals. The screaming woman in the long skirt is detached from the bed end, undressed and laid on her back. Exposed, ashamed, afraid, she screams out of rhythm with her pains. Explanations that would make things easy for her are lost in the confusion of language, culture, religion, ignorance and obstinacy. The doctors are to blame, the nurses, the women, their husbands.

When our daughter had her first baby her husband was there to support her. She timed it so that she was in hospital only an hour before her daughter was born. I rang her in her hospital room an hour or two later. 'I've fed her' she said. 'I've had a shower and I feel good. I watched her being born, all of it. It was a marvellous experience.'

She fed her baby whenever the baby was hungry. Her breasts temporarily were no longer sexual tools, they were her daughter's sustenance, and no more to be hidden than loaves of bread.

I never tasted Joan's milk. That, too, I would do now. But in the immediacy of fatherhood her breasts seemed detached from me. If I touched them the nipples did not stiffen wondrously – they were already erect. What they did was spout milk, three or four high, sticky, continuous jets. It seemed a waste. She had plenty of other parts to kiss.

It is a delight that never palls to watch nipples erect. Each has its separate life. One can rise up in a crimson column fifteen millimetres tall surrounded by a spreading lake of rosy areola while its companion remains collapsed in the centre of a little brown pool. Tease that one too with tongue, with lips. It stiffens. Its skin crinkles. The pool washes outward and lightens in colour. Sometimes the second can be coaxed up with words. 'One up, one to go.' Watch and wait.

Extend the caresses with the hands. The areolae corrugate and thrust the nipples out even longer, stiffer, darker. Suck them. They nourish the spirit.

Photographed frontview breasts look like poached eggs on plates. But in the bath with steaming water washing

Sight

about them breasts and pubic hair are water fern and lotus flowers in a tropic pool.

The vulva is a prodigy. What one sees first is no more than a seam in a furry cushion with its edges outlined by longer denser hairs like the growth of trees along an Australian river bank. Part the hairs. Part the outer lips. There are limp and folded leaves of flesh inside. Let them close and stroke the edges of the seam. Kiss them. Lick them. Murmur against them so one's own lips vibrate. They open, not imperceptibly like a rosebud, but like a sea anemone pulsating as it opens to feed.

And what's that at the top? Two flaps of flesh meet beneath it in a v-shaped signpost. It is the man in the boat, say the Chinese. Or is it a bald-headed Eskimo looking out of his igloo; or a shy little animal that lives in a tunnel? It advances its pink nose. It grows braver and reaches out farther. It becomes the foreman directing the work below, a conductor, or the sorcerer's apprentice who loses control.

The seam widens till it is a glistening pink oval. It deepens, grows rounder. It is a slippery-sided cone dropping into a well with a broken cover. And the formerly unimpressive drapes of flesh surrounding it flare into a scalloped ruff proud as a cock's comb.

The conductor has lost control. He backs off-stage into the corridor like a nervous mouse. And flesh arches above him protectively.

In a pornographic film I watched on a wide screen, an ejaculating penis was suddenly magnified into a two-metre column spurting out of the top of the frame. The jerks were awe-inspiring, the spouts tremendous. One began to wish for an umbrella. As the spouting degenerated to oozing, the collapsing column was moved to the left of the screen and a two-metre cunt in the turmoil of orgasm was presented alongside it. It looked like a geyser in those energetic few minutes before it erupts.

A scene cut from a French film by puritan censors for Australia's timid audiences showed a female cook stirring a thick potato soup. Her right hand moved the wooden spoon round and round, across and back. It scraped and lifted. Her left hand began to beat a tattoo against her groin. Her fingers stroked, circled. She pulled up her frock, pulled

Celebration

down her pants. Her right hand turned a right hand circle, her left hand turned to the left. Both hands increased the vigour of the stirring, left hand leading. The soup began to bubble. The camera moved down to her vulva pouting, winking. She put the lid on the saucepan, pulled up her pants.

Pornographic is a destructive word. What good erotic films do is satisfy one's immense curiosity without involving one. Life is profounder and happier with one vital woman, provided each partner has distinct interests. But how spend a lifetime stirring one vulva with one penis and know no other? And since cocks and cunts are attached to emotions and cannot be detached as specimens, how does one untangle the shemozzle of emotions if one goes in search of experience? Life becomes not delight but devastation. By film one gets experience without involvement. And watching fellow cocks in action is almost as interesting as watching cunts.

In a few hours one meets the concave penis, the convex, the straight, the twisted, the circumcised, the uncircumcised with the prepuce no more than a beret drawn over the corona or a Ku-Klux-Klan hood covering the entire glans, the short and thick, the long and thin, the big-headed, the small-headed, the round, the oval, the smooth, the hairy, the red, black, yellow, brown and grey, the oozers, the squirters, the firers before the slow-motion camera of delicate curling ribbons, the horizontal erections, the vertical, or the penis so long it sagged like a dropped railway signal arm. The two girls who helped the owner of that one demonstrate it laid him on his back and directed it up his belly. It reached centimetres past his navel. They circled it with four hands and the glans projected clearly.

When he began to work it, disadvantages showed up. Neither girl could get much more than half of it in. Nine or ten centimetres throbbed in the cold. Worse it did not seem to get stiff enough. The exposed section kept buckling. One feared it might fatigue and break like a piece of bent wire. It would have looked more comfortable if he had fitted it with a stout spacing washer.

The end of these films is always the unimaginative same. All the penises that have been on view must ejaculate. They

Sight

withdraw to prove it. Semen fills the last frame. So his partner of the moment removed the end that was in her cunt, put as much as she could in her mouth, wrapped both hands round the shaft, and began to suck slowly and massage briskly. At the right moment she presented the primed weapon eye-on to the camera. One expected it to gush like a firehose. Instead two or three feeble spasms yielded reluctant blobs like the last squeezings from a tube of toothpaste.

A Negro performer animated his penis not by humping his back but by flexing the remarkable muscles in his buttocks. Each buttock had a separate control and vibrated at astonishing speed. When he finally withdrew from his partner for the conventional ending, the thick semen rolling down the coal-black pole looked unnaturally white.

Such films are usually made by the unintelligent for the unintelligent. Most of those that satisfy any part of the imagination do so by chance. Vulvas are treated superficially. The cunt is a convenience for the cock, not its equal partner. Still, one sees pubic hair dense, sparse, shaven; outer lips thick and thin, meeting or parted; inner lips long or short, scalloped or plain, matched, unmatched, smooth or wrinkled, dangling or trim. Erected or unerected is an accident of filming time. No one making pornographic films is aware of the difference. The camera often misses the clitoris altogether, that miracle that is a different organ in every woman, not only in its appearance, in its susceptibility.

Except for the parties of young and lonely Japanese students, one abhors one's cinema companions: the old, the ugly, the infirm, the occasional middle-aged businessman carrying his briefcase as a badge, all sitting hunched, separate, furtive. The audience is inexorably male. And too often female dancers come embarrassingly to entertain them. The energetic cocks and cunts black out on the screen, lights flash, music loudens, and a clothed girl appears on stage. Ineptly, absurdly, she kicks about, removes her clothes and to a climactic fanfare stands distant and naked on the stage. The lights go out again and whatever filmed penises were at work in whatever cunts continue to the inevitable climax.

Sometimes as a bonus the girls dance down the first four

Celebration

or five rows of the cinema – men hurry to take seats there – presenting breasts to be stroked, buttocks to be gripped, or fingers to be smelt that have been drawn between the legs. One energetic girl involved the whole audience. She rolled from lap to lap, she somersaulted across the aisles. She put hands on foreheads, nipples in mouths. She presented her cunt to be sucked from the front, from the back. Hands stretched towards her. Men called and coaxed. She took a man on stage, undid his trousers, tried to jerk him off, gave it up as hopeless and came back for more kissing. Her expression never changed. One supposed her cunt was as cold as her eyes. She came too near me. I was carrying a couple of newly-bought records. I held them before me like a shield, prim with fear of herpes, syphilis, gonorrhoea, offended by the assumption I needed to touch her. I left as soon as she rolled past. It is discomforting to go among the starving somewhat too fat and too recently fed.

Intelligent erotic films, imaginative erotic films, might be a joyous exhibition for men and for women. No society, not even the early Marquesan, has happily accommodated sex. It seems more than man is capable of enjoying. He flinches, he fumbles, he frets, he fights, he feels, he frigs, he fucks, he fellates, he forbids, he fantasises, he fails.

See Australia in the 1950s. It was not substantially different to anywhere else in the 1950s. The little that was happening had happened elsewhere or was about to happen. The world was resting after a war: stable, enervated, dull. Our differences were of climate, of language, of casual custom. Belligerent old-fashioned religion is a more modern terror. Modernisation was the chief religion of the 1950s.

New-gashed power lines webbed the countryside. We carted beautiful old kerosene lamps with fluted glass chimneys to the rubbish dump and replaced them with electric bulbs and bakelite shades.

The precise linesmen who had a pole half-way up at five o'clock in the afternoon dropped it lest they work overtime. They hauled it up again at 7.30 the next morning. Fly-by-night electricians towed their caravans from house to country house and installed thick ropes of faulty wiring. The one that came to us left wires dangling out of the wall above Kim's head where a reading light was to go. He assured us the wires were not connected. Floods drowned our finances. There was no money for anything but essentials. It was two years before another electrician installed the light we could at last afford. The wires were live. Kim said he sometimes thought about standing up and sucking them but even at two he decided it might be dangerous.

Corrugated-iron verandahs over country-town shop fronts became unmodern eyesores. Councils ordered them unroofed and the shapely posts removed from the footpaths. Bald redbrick and plate glass walls then replaced the unprotected timber and gave no shelter from sun or rain. Towns like Singleton in New South Wales that preserved many of the old verandahs and weatherboard shop fronts now have singular grace.

We sat on chrome and vinyl chairs at laminex tables. We discarded horses for farm work and grew deaf on tractors. We made the most unimaginative meals in the world out of the best food in the world. Leo Büring, Maurice O'Shea, and Dan Tyrrell made dry red wines different from but equal to the world's best. Those of us who drank it were regarded as foreign and un-Australian. Real men drank rum, beer when they were thirsty. It preceded a good feed: a big, well-done steak with two or three eggs on top accompanied by greasy chips.

Barbers cut our hair short back and sides and our ears stuck out from our heads like gargoyles. When I picked up a pen to write, I considered the censor as much as the sense. I had to, else the work came back – even poems. The books the Government allowed us to read and write were as bare of sex as celluloid dolls. We lived in complacency as thick as syrup.

We talked, some of us, about naked ballet, and swimming naked, and honest books, and of vegetables that were not boiled limp and meat that was not baked dry. Except for the cooking we could do nothing but talk. There is not much life in gaol. Any change, even in the mid-1950s, seemed more than a lifetime away.

The numerical size of the generation that matured only ten years later in the 1960s helped them. They were the

Celebration

bumper after-war crop, modern in morals rather than machinery. There were more than enough to make themselves heard. They came out imaginative, scornful, vigorous and shameless. They reviled the censors and mocked the policemen chasing them with the clothes they had discarded.

The first stage show proving a change was a troupe of African dancers. The girls were bare-breasted and lush. Only in Brisbane were they forced to wear blouses as well as the short skirts they wore everywhere. The nakedness was necessary as well as beautiful else one lost the super-human control they had of their stomach muscles. They sat astride drums and beat them to a lively rhythm. The skin on the left side of their bellies began to circle, then the skin on the right in the opposite direction. They ridged the skin across their waists and rolled the ridge up through their breasts and down again over and over in time to the quickening drums. They acted a crocodile and a sinuous line of bodies writhed about the stage. And they screamed – how they screamed! – as they re-enacted their clitoridectomies. The audience blanched.

Two or three years later the musical *Hair* triggered a more definite change. When Berger made that wild leap out of a box three metres above the stage and hit the boards dancing and searching for Donna, we danced with him into a sensible and exciting new world. For the first time in Australia the puritans were left panting behind. And it appals me that after twelve lively years they might be catching up again led by the Reverend Fred Nile, newly elected to the Legislative Council of the New South Wales Parliament. His supporters frighten me. They give me the impression they would like to cut off my penis and stitch up my gullet as a warning to all those who enjoy themselves.

The brilliant European theatre group, Kiss, or Silk as they called themselves in Australia to distinguish them from the pop group, who came to Melbourne in 1979 were a marvel one never expected to see in the 1950s. They used nakedness or clothes with equal effect. Who else should Eve be but two naked girls tempting Adam with food? They had open bottles of wine between their legs, plastic buckets full of food beside them. In time to music they scooped up double handfuls of cream cake, danced with it to Adam,

Sight

smeared it against his face, crushed it greedily into their mouths when he refused. Cream ran down bellies and legs. Bits of cake snagged in their pubic hair. They splashed Adam with wine, then held the bottles to their mouths and gulped to show him how. Wine dripped from their breasts, stained the cream on their bodies, dribbled across the floor. They pulled hams out of the buckets, bit off chunks and offered them to Adam on their tongues. They crushed raw eggs, slurped them out of their palms, and wiped their hands on Adam's buttocks. The music grew merrier. Adam, the girls, the stage became splattered with food. The Garden of Eden was bountiful.

And what else should God be but an unmoving column of aluminium reflecting coloured lights? When it was necessary he came to life. The column shivered. A long piece broke out of one side, lifted up. A similar piece broke out of the other side. They were arms. The base split, became legs. God walked about. He was a man in silver clothes on two-metre stilts.

In a performance of Aeschylus's *Agamemnon* presented as a ritual by the same group, fourteen naked actors and actresses stood on their heads and sang a chorus in ancient Greek to show that their world was turned upside-down by war. The atmosphere they had built up was so real they did not appear ridiculous. The audience was totally absorbed. The front row of seats circled the actors. The nearest was no more than a metre away.

The Kalakshetra Dancers of Madras who came to Australia in the mid-1960s presented folk dances hundreds of years old and musical plays written last century that seemed as modern as *Hair*. Their discipline, their training is extreme, as exacting as that of classical ballet dancers. Each finger, each toe has to develop separate, distinct, stylised movement. They can turn their heads around farther than normal and they can slide stiffened heads and necks two centimetres or so out of line towards either shoulder. A row of half-a-dozen dancers move their heads together. It looks graceful, not grotesque.

In a very funny folk dance to lively Indian music, seven girls mocked one man with their feet. Individual toes beckoned him, whole feet welcomed him. When he danced before

Celebration

the feet, unable to make up his mind, lifted toes inspected him more closely, lost attention, looked elsewhere. Some toes waved him away, big toes pointed towards the door. He grew braver and tried to approach. Whole feet rejected him, pushed towards him to hold him at a distance. Then all the toes moved as though they were laughing at him. He slunk away out of the door. The toes drummed happily on the floor, the heels thumped, as the girls danced off in the other direction. As each stepped through the door she wiggled her buttocks derisively.

One needs to meet the unaccustomed. Assurance is too soft a bed to get out of quickly. We did not expect to be jarred at a circus in Boggabri where we took the children to see the traditional clowns, the trick ponies, the elephants, the liontamer, the monkeys riding bicycles, the acrobats on the high trapeze. All those were there. But one man walked into the arena carrying two smallish suitcases, obviously light. He swung them as he walked. He put them on a table, opened them up. He reached into one with his right hand, pulled up an arm. It stuck up stiffly. He reached his left hand into the other suitcase, pulled up a leg. He pulled out another arm, another leg. He pulled out a head. What looked like two stiff dolls sat there with arms, legs and heads stuck out at unnatural angles. He grabbed one by a foot, the other by a hand, and threw them both over his shoulders. They landed on their feet as a man and a woman and performed a contortionist act. They were each very slim and short, no more than a metre tall. Their joints were so flexible they seemed to have no bones. They formed themselves into a hoop and rolled across to a pole where they broke apart and coiled up the pole and down it again like a long snake. They climbed ladders by writhing in and out between the rungs. In the end they knotted themselves together, pliable as rope. The man who had carried them in came back with the suitcases, untied them, threw them into the cases, folded down the limbs that stuck out stiffly, closed the lids, and walked out. No one applauded. It was too unreal to clap.

Australia has come to life generally since the 1950s. The landscape below the Tropic of Capricorn – forest, desert and farm – was bared by rabbits. Few wildflowers bloomed,

Sight

few new trees had grown since the 1880s. When the introduced disease myxomatosis destroyed most of the rabbits in the good years of the early 1950s, plants revived. So insects revived and the animals that prey on insects and those that prey on insect-eaters: the cycles of feeders and fed-on accelerated and proliferated. In the lush 1980s one can stand in one place before a little mallee in massed purple flower and count over a hundred species of wasps, bees, flies, moths, butterflies and bugs.

Pollen is a good food for bird and insect. Nectar excites. A halo of ecstasy rings the mallees. They buzz, whisper, hum, whirr, beat, drone, thud with feeding insects. There are blue flies, brown flies, green flies, big flies, little flies, bronze flies, flies with huge yellow heads, flies with tiny orange heads, flies with longitudinal stripes, flies with cross stripes, flies with so many short white hairs on the abdomen they look like blobs of cotton wool. As one of these was feeding, a small red wasp flew in above it, stabbed it and at once began to suck its juices: fortified nectar. There are fast fliers, slow fliers, straight fliers, zig-zaggers, gauzy wings, patterned wings, gay wings, hoverers, crawlers, the minute, middle-sized, big. Some unroll a proboscis over twenty millimetres long and look about as they suck. Others with no proboscis at all dive headfirst down to the nectar. Some feed restlessly, some feed soberly at the one flower for minutes. Some feed frenziedly – their abdomens throb – and mate briefly and unconcernedly.

Some of the lone native bees are brilliant: black bees with yellow heads, black bees with bright blue dots, glossy amber bees, brown bees with metallic green stripes, big bees with a pair of crimson pockets on their rear legs for storing pollen. They carry it to their individual honey pots in holes in the ground or in trees. Some bees sport weird extensions from heads or thoraxes. One has a little black flag on a twelve-millimetre pole. It waves it as it feeds.

Long, thin, winged males of a bug tow behind them their short, plump, wingless females joined in an unenthusiastic mating. The males feed hurriedly and seem oblivious of the females that get buried in blossom, scraped over leaves, bumped against stems in flight from branch to branch.

Celebration

Here and there a praying mantis waits, unobtrusive as a leaf, unthreatening, but the barbed front legs are folded ready to strike and hold.

Ploughing in the early morning, slicing through the long shadows of the rising sun, involves one in the chaos of creation. I unmake to make. Wildflowers are about to open, the grass is crisp, dew marks out the intricate webs of orb-weaving spiders. The first cut of the discs overturns all that. One looks behind on dead soil. Can sun and rain reanimate it? One circles the paddock, follows the furrow into the next spiral. To the east over the first ploughed ground, light glints on web. Every square metre is meshed with glistening new lines. In twenty minutes tiny spiders have crawled from where they were buried and spun themselves something familiar in an unknown landscape. To find them one has to sift soil and search with a high-powered lens. It is easier to believe the very crumbs of soil have come to life and drifted web into the sunlight.

The glass-walled, air-conditioned cabs of modern tractors are superior seats in a natural theatre. Machinery, even noisy machinery, does not worry animals much. Life goes on as if one had not intruded except that the dust of cultivation, like smoke, attracts many birds. They know well it means disturbance, unwary behaviour and easy prey.

I plough paddocks of good soil studded with Kurrajongs, shapely trees with glossy dark-green leaves. There is an occasional tall native pine among them or a scant-leaved eucalypt. The Kurrajongs are good cover for small birds, the others good lookouts for hawks.

The eaters of worms and grubs work behind the plough. Half a dozen ravens strut the furrow. Small flocks of magpies, a hundred or so black and white peewits search the broken ground. They probe with beaks, rake with their feet. Often they stop, watch and listen. A magpie will approach a propped-up clod, bend low, turn its head on one side, peer beneath and reach in cautiously with open beak. But if it has to reach so far it risks dislodging the clod on its head, it withdraws carefully, plants its feet firmly, braces its legs and with beak and neck as lever overturns the clod. It snaps quickly and moves on.

Sight

The small insect-eaters, pipits, bushlarks, Willie Wagtails, several species of wood-swallows, eat flying insects mostly and they move haphazardly between tree and grass, between ploughed and unploughed ground. There is plenty for them to eat, they are fearless about exposing themselves. Their diet makes them unpalatable. Wood-swallows and Willie Wagtails demonstrate this. If a Little Eagle, a Brown Falcon, a Little Falcon, even a giant Wedge-tailed Eagle finds a suitable lookout on top of the Kurrajong small birds are using as an insect-hunting base, both species attack with what seems astounding courage. Willie Wagtails persist longer than wood-swallows. A pair of wagtails will buffet a Little Falcon with their wings, peck at its head, dive on it, hover in front of it chattering. The Little Falcon, a supreme hunter, could simply lift one foot and pluck the nuisance out of the air. But what would it do then? Once those curved talons, three in front, one behind, lock in flesh and bone, the only way the falcon can get them free again is by eating whatever they are holding. A Willie Wagtail would make three or four nasty mouthfuls. So the great hawks bear with their tormentors long enough to demonstrate unconcern, then they fly off to a quieter lookout.

The male Brown Songlark with his harem of six or seven half-sized females ignores everything but himself. The females, anonymous as the soil, feed busily. He sings. I cannot hear him when the engine is going but I can see his open beak and know that he is pouring out a loud, creaky, metallic song as though a music box is playing inside a tin bird. Even the way his silvery wings glitter as he jerks about in the air looks mechanical. Now and then he drops carelessly on to something he has seen during the singing, his beak opens and shuts, snap, like the flap on an old-fashioned money box, then he rises again whirring. The light flutters through his wings. He is a little silver helicopter.

It is the several species of quail that are troubled by the ploughing. They are grain-eaters and so palatable all but the biggest hawks and eagles seek them. In lush seasons when the crops of wheat and barley grow tall and flaggy then fall over as they ripen into tangled masses, quail come to us in thousands. There is grain to eat and superb cover. They move through colonnades of stems beneath arches of brown

Celebration

leaves. Harvest is the first disruption. Combine harvesters lift the mat of straw in swaths, cut it off and elevate it into corrugated drums spinning over concave systems of bars and mesh that thresh the grain from the heads. A further system of wind blasts and shaking sieves in each machine separates the grain from the broken mass of straw, hulls and dust. The grain is elevated into a bin, the waste drops in a thick wide line out of the back of the machine. And among that waste are many dead quail that have been swept into the machine as they tried, too late, to lift out of the straw. At every stop one finds two or three warm crumpled bodies lying on the sieves. And I cannot reconcile the sorrow I feel to see them there with the eagerness I regard quail on my dinner plate, boned, stuffed with *pâté de foie gras* and truffles, cooked in butter, masked with Madeira sauce.

American farmers often bale their fluffy windrows of cured lucerne hay at night when the moister air lessens leaf shatter. Nesting pheasants, asleep on their eggs laid under what seemed the protection of the hay, are pressed into the bales. No one knows until a bale is opened and a bouquet of bones and gay feathers falls to ground.

After several weeks, when the quail have readjusted to nearby grass paddocks or whatever cover they could find in the stubble paddocks, there is the second awful disruption of ploughing. The little button-quail suffer the most. They are a convenient size for several species of hawks. Their lives are threatened by shadows. Even the edge of a cloud-shadow causes a running quail to freeze until it realises no hawk could be so big, then it relaxes and moves again. But the black form of a sharp pair of wings is the definite shape of death. When that shadow glides over its back, a quail might freeze for an hour.

The tractor and plough force them to move. Some again leave it too late. I do not always see them or declutch in time. The discs catch them, cut them in half or bury them alive. Sometimes I look back to see a male quail running in circles about the clods and turned soil, scratching quickly, running again. He can hear his buried young ones, fully feathered and active from the time he hatched them – the male is keeper of the brood – crying under the surface. And

Sight

frequently he digs some up unharmed, five or six perhaps, out of eight, nine, or ten.

But most of the quail fly out on to the ploughed ground. They behave as though it is a fire approaching when bare ground is the lesser peril.

Two Brown Falcons regularly attend our ploughing. When they are really hungry they leave their vantage points in the trees and glide in spirals a hundred metres or so above the tractor. As a quail takes off on its low, fast, straight, one-or-two-hundred-metre flight, the nearer falcon dives. Sometimes it times its dive perfectly and plucks the quail out of the air. Usually it dives short and has to chase the quail. The wings of the Brown Falcon are pointed and swept back. It looks as though it is built for speed, and so it is, but it is the slowest of the falcons. If there is a handy timber belt or grassy fence line, the quail can outfly the falcon to safety. But after about three hundred metres a quail tires. The falcon gains. As it accelerates for the strike, the quail plummets into the ground like a stone and freezes. The falcon marks where it is, fans its wings, turns in the air as it brakes, glides back, hovers, drops and strikes. Often the quail has cleverly moved a few centimetres while the falcon was turning. Then the talons clutch dirt. The falcon knows the quail is within grasp but it cannot see it unless the quail moves. It rakes with its feet, opens and shuts its beak, makes little cackling noises, pecks towards the ground. It jumps in the air and throws out its wings. It makes short rushing movements. If the quail can keep its nerve and not move it has a chance. But as the terrible beak bends over them or the talons rake the ground beside them, most quail hurtle into the air and the falcon nonchalantly stretches out a foot and clasps them.

Our Little Eagle, a sturdy bird patterned in cream and brown, keeps watch effortlessly by gliding round within the thermals a few hundred metres up. Only the bigger prey attracts it. If a young hare is flushed into the open, the eagle watches it as it runs a little way, cringes, tries to hide under an upturned weed, moves on. Then the eagle comes down on it in a calm, decisive swoop and eats it on the ground.

I watched from a hide as a Little Eagle came to water at

Celebration

the only waterhole left in a big, droughty forest. A lot of birds, mostly parrots and honeyeaters, were watering there. There were a few sharp alarm calls, a quick withdrawal from water to cover, then separate alarm calls from every species of bird about. The Little Eagle flew in slowly, landed unnecessarily high up on the bank, fluffed his feathers, preened himself a little, looked about. Only a Willie Wagtail chattered and hopped along the water's edge looking for insects. Every other bird was still and quiet. After several minutes' intimidation the eagle stepped down to water, important as a politician. He *proceeded* to the water. Then for all of fifteen minutes he dipped his beak slowly, scooped up water, lifted his head, tilted it back for long intervals while the water ran down his gullet, dipped again. Then he flew away. Birds began to chatter again, to sing. Some flew down to water, thirsty but very wary. So the eagle returned, made a low, slow triumphant circuit of the pool that panicked all the birds again, then flew off till the next day's performance.

The big Spotted Harrier, handsome blue-grey and chestnut, that flies slow, metre-high transects up and down our paddocks, causes little panic. It does eat quail if they present themselves carelessly. It prefers mice and baby hares. It settles beside them, strikes calmly, swallows them in two or three bites, then continues its course. At the boundary fence, strangely, it turns. It is our bird, and seldom leaves the farm.

A pair of Little Falcons will follow a tractor for hours. They are fast and spectacular. In a folded-wing plunge one will snatch a grasshopper as it rises directly before the front wheel of the tractor, eat it as it glides above the cab, turn and dive as the next grasshopper rises.

A male button-quail with seven or eight young ones, so newly hatched they were unwilling to fly, tried to bustle them along the furrow as the tractor approached. They could run about five kilometres an hour, not the nine kilometres the tractor was travelling. The male pretended to be wounded to distract the attention of the monster that was chasing them. He fluttered clumsily in the air, fell, ran for a metre, rose again, fell. A blue arrow hit him as he rose again and the Little Falcon glided to the top of a tall box

Sight

tree. It bent over, grasped a tuft of feathers, threw them into the air, then tore into flesh. Before the scatter of little feathers reached the ground, the quail was eaten, the falcon was on the wing again.

The great Warrumbungle Mountains we live near, and their broken extensions on to tree-covered flats, are the most important breeding-grounds left in the world for the Peregrine Falcon. These world-wide rangers can dive at two hundred kilometres an hour, take an animal weighing half a kilogramme off the ground and lift it without hesitation, without touching ground, and with little loss of speed. One marvels that feathers can stand the strain of such a turn. All one sees is a blurred, blue-grey V. But sometimes I see young Peregrine Falcons learning to hunt on their own, persistent, inept, hungry enough to be undignified. One flew towards a flock of twenty-odd peewits feeding on the ground near a Kurrajong. As it climbed to dive, one of the peewits saw it. It squawked an alarm call and the flock raced for cover deep within the leaves. So the young falcon dived slowly at the tree, fluttered about it, beat leaves with its wings, grasped branches and shook them. It rose and dived again, screaming on the way down, then circled the tree in tight spirals, screaming all the while. Nothing it did frightened the birds into breaking cover but it tried for half an hour before it gave up and sought other game. And peewits are not choice prey. As occasional grain-eaters hawks sometimes take them, but they eat so many insects nothing favours them.

The vibrations of a tractor engine attract the big black cicadas that live in the forest to the north of our boundary. They circle the exhaust pipe, sometimes so wildly they stun themselves against it. Occasionally one flies below the centrifugal air cleaner and gets sucked into the perspex bowl. I watch it spinning in the dust, catching hold sometimes, spinning again. I watch it for half a round, one round, then I become the one being spun. I turn off the engine, unscrew the cover and let it fly away.

When tractor-driving at night the world is the sphere of the lights. One is allowed a censored view of the paddock so surprises are few and memorable. Once a Fat-tailed Sminthopsis ran in front of the tractor. She was lumpy and

Celebration

odd-looking with seven young ones clinging to the fur on her back and sides. They are pretty creatures, about the size of a House Mouse, patterned in grey and white. The wide tail stores fat to tide them over lean times. She jumped down into the furrow then out on to the worked ground and headed for the darkness. As she sprang out of the furrow one of the young ones fell off. I stopped the tractor and picked it up. It squeaked. The mother heard and ran back to claim it. I held my hand with the young one in it close to the ground. She stopped a few centimetres away, chattered a little, then hopped up into my palm. The young one scrambled on to her back again and she turned and ran for the comforting darkness.

Years before a leveret ran before me in the furrow one night. It was no more than a day or two old. Bewildered by the light and the noise, it was unwilling to leave the furrow, a good unobstructed path, even though I slowed down several times. When it was obviously tiring I stopped the tractor to catch it and move it out of the way. As I approached, it ran into the protection of the deep shadow under the front tractor wheel and flattened itself between tyre and ground. I picked it up by the loose skin at the back of the neck. It cried out sharply and astonishingly loudly for such a small animal. At once there was a heavy thumping not far away in the darkness. It frightened me. It sounded like a big animal and there should have been no big animals in the paddock. The baby hare cried out again. It was answered by more thumping, then the sound of something running towards me. Whatever it was out there was charging.

Into the circle of light came the mother hare. She ran on her front legs, stepped high with her back legs and drummed the full length of the shank on the ground with every step. The noise was as loud as a galloping horse. She ran right up to me and smelled at her young one in my hand. It cried out again. The mother leapt in the air, thudded both shanks on the ground, then stood up, held out her fore paws for balance and worked her hind legs alternately in a frenzied tattoo that increased in speed and loudness. Her legs blurred. No jazz drummer ever moved his sticks so fast.

I released her baby. She stopped, dropped on to four

Sight

feet, leant forward and wrinkled her nose over it, licked it a few times, then led it off quietly into the night.

Interesting as animals are, man makes the more entertaining pageant. Animals are never absurd, rarely comic. Absurdity is built into mankind with self-consciousness. Attend a monthly barbecue of an East-Asian Art Society in a southern Australian city.

About sixty people altogether gathered in a pleasant backyard. There were Japanese faces and Malay, Chinese and part-Chinese, European, Indonesian and some indeterminable. All stood about the garden in small groups talking and drinking beer out of cans, or flagon red out of glasses if they had arrived early, out of paper cups if they had not. Steak and sausages charred on a battery of five or six low briquette-fired grids set down temporarily on the lawn. Now and then the wind changed and the smell of burning fat shifted people and reorganised the groups.

Three tall women walked about with trays of biscuits and bowls of savoury mush to dip them in. They moved aimlessly like caged peahens. Make-up was smudged on and their dress careless. They might have been at the beginning of moult.

'I adore Chinese painting' one told me. 'There is nothing like it.' She was impractically arty. 'But we had to extend our interests. There were so few of us in the beginning. So now we do Japanese painting, too, and flower-arranging. And some of our newest members are interested in Thailand, and some in... oh! I think *I* adore all things Asian.'

'It's language that brings me here' said another as she passed. 'I'm good at language, you know. I did Japanese for three years and I just soaked it up. I'm the sort of student tutors like to have in a class. But then I was so fluent I felt I needed another interest. So I've just finished a year of Chinese and I'm continuing next semester. The characters are a dream.' Her voice grew husky. 'They really get you in.'

'What are you going to do with these languages?'

'I'll never use them. That was not the intention. It's just an interest, you know.'

The first grid-fulls of steak and sausages cooked. People

Celebration

began to collect plates, drinks, and select their meat. Some sat in the few chairs and ate conveniently, some sat on the lawn. But the lawn was a cold place to sit, so many stood, looked helplessly at both laden hands, then put glasses on the lawn at their feet, held plate and useless knife and fork with the left hand and began to pick up their food with the right.

Four Chinese students, sent out from Beijing for two years to perfect their good English at an Australian university, sat beside one another in chairs. They managed their steaks clumsily and noisily. Not yet accustomed to knife and fork, each would cut off too big a square, spear it through the middle with a fork, then hold it up and turn it slowly while he chewed his way around the four sides. This technique looks neat when a well-braised chicken bone is held in a pair of chopsticks. The flesh slips easily and a couple of deft half-turns allow the teeth to bare the bone nicely. But a fork is an ugly instrument held upright in a hammer grip. And a piece of medium-rare steak becomes nastily ragged and bloody on the third round of bites.

The student who sat next to me was discomfited by his first Australian barbecue and by the uncut meat which he found gross. Up till then the four of them had been preparing their own meals in Australia. He told me he had a wife and son in Beijing and would not see them again for two years. He missed his son – he showed his photograph. But he had no photograph of his wife. 'In China we love our children more than our wives.'

Perhaps his wife reminded him of the sliced Chinese food he was missing. He waved his fork with a soggy remnant on it. 'This is an Australian barbecue, yes?' The yes was punctuation. He answered himself with a falling tone, 'Ye-es. In China we do not do it this way. We do not all stand about, yes. We like to meet in homes in groups of ten to twelve and we all sit down, yes, at a big table and we eat and talk. In China we do not like it this way.'

In a little Italian restaurant in Wellington, New Zealand, I watched a slight pretty Italian girl and her gross partner eating spaghetti. She speared a few long strands at a time, twirled her fork rapidly till the last end rolled up, then slipped a neat coil into her mouth. He was a big man and fat. He took his fork in an overhand grip, stabbed it into the centre of the piled bowl, lifted an untidy bunch to his mouth, put the fork down, laid both his hands flat on the table, bent over and sucked. Spaghetti writhed out of the bowl, twisted itself into a narrow column and disappeared upward into his mouth. It was a waterspout of spaghetti. His face was the cloud, the bowl the sea. The column showed no sign of breaking but he paused two or three times before the plate was empty. He just stopped sucking, chopped his teeth together and the lopped-off column fell back on itself till he was ready to begin again.

Universal, pleasurable, necessary, frequent, public – few eat alone – eating is an ideal target for the imposers of law and order, so it is set about with taboos and convention in all societies. When I was very young I was taught that if I put my knife and fork down during a meal they should be set at a slight angle with the prongs of the fork turned down. That showed the waiter I had not finished eating. Knife and fork together with the prongs turned up signified my plate might be taken.

Fifty years ago each hotel in a country town was a model of every other hotel in every other town. There was the same smell of fresh beer and stale urine, the same narrow stairs to the bedrooms on the first floor, the same lumpy kapok pillows, the same bathrooms with deep, stained porcelain baths and green brass taps at the end of timber-panelled corridors, the same podgy waitress, the same cook with the same menu. But there was also the same thick, squared verandah posts with rope marks on them where horses were still hitched. And the first floor verandah the big posts held up had a guard of exquisite wrought iron around it.

I was dining with my parents at such a hotel. I had five mouthfuls left: the best slice of roast beef I had kept till last. I put my knife and fork down with calculated correctness while I turned round to examine the other diners. Some of their ways of eating were worth watching. When I turned back to my plate, it was gone. The kitchen door swung behind the waitress. Ever since, irrespective of where my knife and fork is, I keep close watch on an unfinished plate.

More ludicrously there is the formality of bed-making.

Celebration

Even moderate housewives scorn an unmade bed, and with reason. It is uninviting. It threatens rest. What a good broad expanse a well-made double bed is! I sort papers on ours, two or three chapters of a book at a time: photocopies, newspaper clippings, notebooks, stapled printed papers, letters and their answers – two or three hundred perhaps – big brown envelopes full of handwritten notes on strips of paper, tapes of interviews, thirty or forty books. I sit so much more comfortably than on the floor. I read, I sort, I pile, I print tags with a big felt pen and indicate subjects, chapters, dates. All the material for a couple of months writing fits comfortably at once on a double bed. A sixth of a book can lie there waiting to be woken.

Rather than make the bed when I am alone I work on the floor. How unsuitable for sorting an unmade bed is! The piles rise on an uneven base. When only sixty centimetres high they collapse into one another and disorder the chronology. Sheets of paper fold themselves invisibly into creases. Paper clips snag in blankets. Books creep under pillows, lost till bedtime.

But apart from the convenience and the appearance of made beds there is a superstition of bed-making, once stronger than it is now. Coloured sheets were unseemly, too frivolous for serious sleep. Only white sheets ensured pure sleep. Each sheet had to be laid in ordained position: rough side of the hem down, narrow hem to the foot, wide hem to the bedhead. To reverse such a sheet in my mother's day was unthinkable, almost as though one was willing to sleep with head next to a pair of feet.

Modern hospitals maintain an old formality in bed-making. Mattresses must be packaged impeccably in sheets, blankets and cover. If the cover has a ward number or hospital crest stencilled on it, each sister-in-charge decrees where that crest shall face as dogmatically as a compass. The patients make untidy bumps in the neatness.

At a training camp in Queensland during World War II, I struck a major who was a master of formal bed-making. We slept six to a tent, three to each side, on portable board floors. By seven o'clock each morning our palliasses had to be folded three times and placed against the tent wall so that the single fold faced the centre of the tent. Then we

Sight

took up one of our two blankets, held it north-south and folded it lengthways so that the fold faced west. That meant those on each side of the tent folded their blankets opposite ways. Next we folded it from the end alternately forward and back so that when we placed it on top of the palliasse two single edges lay on the bottom, two doubled edges on top. The long folding of the second blanket had to be reversed so that when it was put on top of the first blanket, the double edges mated. It was a miracle of symmetry. The major regularly inspected his design. In one hundred and twenty-three tents, one thousand four hundred and seventy-six blankets sat in seven hundred and thirty-eight pairs, folded edges to the west, single edges to the east, and facing either north or south according to which side of the tent they were on, from top to bottom, two single edges, four double edges, two single edges.

In front of this sculpture of bedclothes we stood our kit-bags, lined-up by one of us from outside the tent, seven-eighths full, stuffed to rotundity, no bulging, no sagging, no lolling against the palliasses. Square on top we sat our tin helmets; about the body we draped whatever webbing haversacks we were not using during the day; at the foot, polished to a mirror finish, we set out our spare pair of boots.

We were six weeks overtrained. We were awaiting shipment. We were mad with energy, vicious with sexual frustration. We marched out each day for more training we did not need, cocky, irreverent, cynical, fighting boredom with every possible weapon. And when we were threatened for catcalling – 'Left, right! Left, right!' for example, 'They can fuck me all day and bloody night but they'll never make me love the baby!' – we thought of the sober lines of dummies back in the tents, irreproachable, obedient, untiring, uncomplaining, unthinking, sexless, the ideal underlings.

In some households there is still a litany of darning socks: a hole demands the response of interwoven stitches. Modern socks are so long-lasting darning is not necessary. But I do not discard my socks on the first hole. When the right big toe wears through, what it makes is a left-foot sock. Often both socks are clearly left-foot, right-foot. They might serve another month or two that way. Then one day one toe, both toes even, strangle themselves in new holes. My prudence is satisfied. The socks can be burnt.

We lived once on dark-chocolate self-mulching river flats that extended to black plains. There was no richer soil. The river threaded the farm with life: fish, birds, water-plants, trees. We loved the farm on the river. But it was no fun being in the river when wild brown water flowed ten kilometres wide. After twenty years and a dozen or more floods, the river began to threaten us. When it was so low it was almost stagnant, when it soaked up the sun like a lagoon and grew algae, weeds, shellfish, when the fish were so fat they would not bite and turtles sunned themselves on every log, when water rats chased one another's tails in late afternoon and startled mayflies with ringing water, when water spiders skimmed from bank to bank, when yabbies tunnelled into the mud, even then from somewhere in its depth the river croaked 'I'll fool you. I'll fool you. If you stay I'll drown you'.

So we sold out and bought a bigger farm on sandy loam scattered with Kurrajongs and White Cypress Pines and the biggest Rough-barked Apples I have ever seen. It was edged and crossed with thickly timbered strips where ground orchids massed in the summer and other wildflowers massed in their season. There were more birds than I had known existed.

The good soil had different qualities to the soil we knew, taking in water more slowly, yielding more of it back, growing plants less quickly, less luxuriantly, but more certainly, and fattening cattle superbly.

'I don't see how this soil will ever grow anything' Joan said, shortly after the move. 'It doesn't take in water fast enough.' She was pissing carelessly up a little slope and back-pedalling out of the flow that was about to swamp her boots. On self-mulching soil one can piss uphill with impunity. It is greedy for water.

Self-mulching soils loosen themselves as they dry out. When wet they are as sticky and intractable as molasses, when dry they are as fluffy as eiderdown. The top six centimetres can be raked through the fingers. If a drop of water falls on the surface, one or two crumbs absorb it immedi-

Sight

ately. They swell. Multiply the drop by a shower of rain. The whole surface of the ground swells. It rises to meet the rain. If the shower persists, the lower crumbs lift the surface in tiny bumps. The ground rolls about, rejoicing in the rain.

When these soils dry right out in a prolonged drought, they shrink and crack open in zigzag gashes. A crack might be six metres deep or more and fifteen centimetres wide. Young lambs fall down them. Horses break their legs in them. Fence posts lean drunkenly, supported by the wires they are meant to support. Sometimes a narrower crack gets stuffed with dry grass, dusted over with soil.

About the year I was born a bullock-team pulled up on the black plain I owned as a man. It was hot and dry. Most of the bullocks lay down in yoked pairs to rest. The two big leaders, roan Shorthorns, stayed on their feet. 'I rode over to talk to the driver' the old former manager of the station told me, 'and just as I got there the nearside leader began to piddle.' The penis of a bull or bullock is folded in a tight S-bend. A bull can straighten this out and he pisses quickly in big, spurting jets. A bullock, a castrated bull, loses the power to protrude his penis. The bend restricts him to a tedious dribble. It collects on the long hairs on his prepuce and drops off in a barely continuous flow. Since a big working-bullock drinks up to one hundred litres of water a day, he needs time to dispose of the waste. 'I was talking to the driver for at least twenty-five minutes' the old manager continued, 'and all the while that bullock kept piddling. And when he finished he had nothing to show for it. He must have been standing over a dusted-up crack. All there was under him was a tiny hole, about the size a black ant would make.'

I walked across one of our flooded paddocks three days after it had been covered with sixty centimetres of water. Before the flood that followed immediately on a long drought the paddock had been gashed open as though by an earthquake. Near where I remembered seeing the widest crack, I heard loud gurgling noises. Water still poured down it in one place. It was as though a big plug had been removed. The funnel of swirling water was forty centimetres wide at the top. Where was it all going, millions of litres? Had the dome of the underworld split open?

Celebration

One of the marvels of Australia is the flooding of a dry creek bed. Thomas Mitchell, the explorer, longed to see it. On his trips through western New South Wales he watched for storms, he questioned Aborigines. In the end he saw a flood come down, and it was not as he imagined it would be. No one who has seen it has imagined it correctly. They expect water to behave like water, to see a Bondi wave channelled down a creek bed.

I have seen a wall of water leave a flooded river and race across country, our country. The ground was already soaked. There was nothing to impede the flow, and that wave behaved like water. It was about seventy centimetres high and it travelled at twenty to thirty kilometres an hour. When it came to a fence it threw it in the air, then rolled it flat beneath it. It roared like water on the move.

Water comes down a creek with swishing noises and the cracking of sticks. It comes so slowly it does not seem natural that the wall of water in the lead can hold itself upright. It might be a metre tall. At its base a tongue twenty centimetres wide, eight centimetres high, protrudes like the flange on the foot of a snail. This tongue has to fill the creek bed, often through two to three metres of dry sand. Since it slides easier on water as a snail slides on its slime, it moves only as quickly as the sand can swallow water. As well, it lifts and feeds into the wall logs, sticks, leaves, grass, carcasses, the accumulation of perhaps seven or eight years. The litter tosses about slowly on the wall before it is engulfed. Sticks jut forward, poke up into the air. Some are carried metres in the one position. They look as though they have been prodded into honey.

In front of this creeping semi-solid wall there is an unchanged dry creek bed. Behind it there is a creek full of brown water with a barely perceptible current.

Water fascinates me because it presents the unexpected. Under the relentless mass of atmosphere, in the great hold of gravity, it could lie in sulky puddles, placid lakes, dead seas. Earthquakes heave it into disorder, the moon quickens it, wind plays with it. A grazier began to set up a tractor-driven pump beside what looked like a well-filled western lake. There was a good north wind blowing. He had to run a pipeline three or four kilometres to the paddock he

Sight

wanted to water. Before he had finished the job, the wind had swung to the south and driven the water five kilometres away to the other side of the flat lake bed. When the wind dropped, the water would spread out a few centimetres deep until another wind bunched it up and chased it into a corner.

Along the east coast of the South Island of New Zealand the moon pulls the flood tide north. The North Island turns much of this water and it pours west through Cook Strait, the windpipe of the Pacific Ocean. At the first opportunity, and for no obvious reason, it swings south past Cape Jackson and Alligator Head. A twenty-kilometre strip of wild water tries to fit between D'Urville Island and the mainland through a hundred-metre gap in a jagged reef, the wing bone of a giant cormorant, according to Maori legend, that tired and died as it buffeted the tide.

The pass is a marvel of moving water. It is known as French Pass because Dumont d'Urville's little *Astrolabe* lost wind at a critical time and spun giddily through it in 1827. I went there years ago to see the favourite waters of Pelorus Jack, the dolphin that met the island steamers, and played about them as they raced to get to the Pass at change of tide. I wrote a long poem about him that was only good in parts. But the trip itself was not unsuccessful: it taught me how to get information. And it left me sights to wonder at ever since.

When the flood tide roars south, the water on the northern side of the reef is half a metre higher than the water on the south side. The noise is so loud one talks with difficulty to a man standing next to one. It does not sound like water, more like traffic on an impossibly busy highway. Where the water spreads out on the southern side, two wide V-shaped counter currents run back into the torrent. Water moving south at nine and a half knots joins water moving north at six knots. The edges meet in a torn ridge about fifty centimetres high. Cross-currents disorder everything. Whirlpools form and disintegrate. Some distance away, just where one begins to feel safe in a little boat, a giant whirlpool spins until the tide changes. It will take down a man and a boat – it has taken down too many men and too many boats. And it has returned neither bone nor broken timber.

I went round D'Urville Island in a little launch with the

Celebration

Maori boatman who had the mail run. He was a master of the seas. It was a windy day and the waves were huge, often six metres or more high on the north-east corner. We saw the world in surges. Sometimes we seemed to be at the bottom of the sea, and the waves above us threatened to break and hold us there. On the southern side of the island the sea was calmer and I could watch the island. On one steep green headland a Red Deer stepped out of cover on to a patch of grass. He threw up his head. We looked up at him so steeply his antlers were outlined against the sky. The spread exaggerated into a flash of jagged black lightning. He dropped his head suddenly to feed. It seemed the action should have somersaulted him into the water. Instead he heard the beat of the launch. He lifted his great head again, listened for a while, smelt the air, then turned easily and galloped to cover.

On such a slope sheep feed safely to the edge, then lose the courage to turn. Some back out eventually; some starve and drop off. A bull has been seen trying to mount a cow facing too steeply uphill. As his front legs lifted and his penis protruded, he somersaulted backwards and crashed three hundred metres into the sea.

At full throb of the engine the mail launch could do eight knots. We came through the pass against the main flood travelling one and a half knots faster than we were. The mailman used the water sheltered by the reef till his launch reached full speed; he turned towards one of the counter currents at an acute angle, bucked over the ridge, turned again, and aimed at the awful rock on the western edge of the pass. The current's speed was added to our own. We charged at it at fourteen knots. When it seemed its stone bayonets must gut us, when surely no counter-thrust was possible, the mailman looked up from the comic he was reading, spun his helm, and we were out in the main current, climbing a hill of water. Our way carried us barely clear of the rock. The launch shuddered. Before we could be swept backwards, the mailman swung the launch to port and we edged along the lesser current on the northern side of the reef until the current slackened, then we headed into open water and made easily for home.

I went out at all stages of the tide in a fast five-metre

Sight

fishing boat with a home-fitted inboard motor. We drifted, we fished with slabs of half-rotten fish on big hooks, and we caught New Zealand Snapper weighing five or six kilogrammes. They picked up the bait gently like a little fish and teased the line out slowly for six metres or so, then they swallowed the bait and tugged like sharks. They did not look like the snapper I knew. Even at that weight they lacked the great bump on the head an old-man snapper develops in Australian waters. Probably they are a different species, even their habits are different; but no scientist has yet distinguished them. And using double-hooked lines and strips of fresh undersized Blue Cod as bait, we pulled in superb Blue Cod two at a time. Fine-grained, white and fragrant, this is one of the best of all fish.

Once I caught a Hag Fish, an eel-like creature about fifty centimetres long. We towed it to a little beach and stranded it on the sand. From pores along its back and sides it began to froth. It covered itself with bubbles of slime. They rose into a mound that kept on growing, buckets and buckets of it, an impossible amount of sticky mucus that will not wash off. An unknowing fisherman has taken one into a little dinghy and had it filled like a bubble bath with the abominable excretion.

Our fishing was not sport. The waters were too dangerous for refined angling. We fished to catch fish. On the ebb tide when fishing was best we made long drifts towards the French Pass reef. If the fisherman had a bite at the last minute, he was reluctant to drop his lines to start the engine. Once, when we were two metres from the reef, the engine misfired. He cranked again. The rocks were bruising us when the engine started. The water is so cold no one can live in it for long. He allowed it too close an opportunity to claim us.

During the few weeks I was at French Pass, an 18-metre low-hulled English naval boat took tidal readings every hour. It was fitted with twin 112 KW engines, a powerful little boat kept in traditional immaculate order. The captain calculated the flow of the tide from the engine revolutions necessary to hold his craft steady in the centre of the pass. When reading the flood tide it took about a quarter of an hour to go through the pass, skirt the worst of the

Celebration

whirlpools, turn and come back for the reading. The captain found he could save this time by swinging the boat stern on to the pass several boat-lengths away, then making a controlled drift into position. He practised till he had the movement perfect. He taught his mate. He left him to take one of the readings at full flood while he filmed it from the shore.

I walked with the captain down the ninety-nine steep narrow steps that lead to the lighthouse on the shore side of the pass. He set up his tripod and camera at an excellent vantage point. He was ready as his boat approached. What he filmed left him white and trembling. The mate misjudged the turn by one boat-length. A cross-current pushed the bow full circle. An opposite cross-current hit the stern. Helm and screws were powerless. The boat spun all the way through the pass and for a hundred metres beyond it. Then the water gave back control to the engines. The mate made his reading. The captain decided it would be wise not to develop his film.

The water is in such turmoil, the change of tide takes place several fathoms down before it takes place on top. So, as the change of flow on top approaches, the water level has balanced itself each side of the reef. For five minutes four times a day the water is still and silent. One cannot even suspect the rage below. It is insulated from the world like a padded cell. One sees flat water. One hears the birds. One hears the cicadas, and they are astonishingly shrill when one realises they could not be heard before. Then the traffic of currents starts on top again. They roar.

At one slack water at low tide I was walking down the lighthouse steps. I heard splashing and loud cracking noises, and I hurried on down to see where they were coming from. A shoal of snapper were chewing mussels off rocks exposed in about forty-five centimetres of water. I could see them all. The sea was in pink bloom with them. Tails waved in the air as some fed upside down with their mouths below water. Others threw heads and fins out of the water and crunched mussels thirty centimetres up the rocks. There were over a hundred of them – I could count them roughly. The water was not deep enough anywhere to cover them as they fed. All were about the one size, fifteen kilogrammes in

Sight

weight, seventy-five centimetres long. They splashed continually to keep themselves wet. Some bit at big bunches of mussels and worried them like dogs, shaking their heads till they broke them free. They fed in a frenzy. They had five minutes to gather what they could before wild water would sweep them out.

Once we lived on a river that showed us all its fish. I had been told when I went there that fish had to come to the surface to breathe if a very muddy rise came down. I watched for it. Each of the other four members of the family watched for it when they joined me. I waited twenty years. In the end we all saw it for one hour. The marvellous does not happen often.

The rise was about three-quarters of a banker. The water was creamy brown. It looked thick. I noticed a few shrimps on the edge, just here and there at first. More came to the bank, and more. They built an unbroken mass of shrimps all along the water's edge, a crust twenty-five centimetres wide, sixteen centimetres deep. It churned about as those underneath struggled to the surface. Yabbies heaved their way through it: black yabbies, blue yabbies, brown yabbies, yabbies three centimetres long, yabbies thirty centimetres long. They propped themselves up on the shrimps. Their black, round, hard little eyes stared at nothing. Their claws worked spasmodically and uselessly. They picked up shrimps, crushed them, dropped them, picked up more. A fish opened its mouth occasionally behind the shrimps, chopped at the air a few times, then dived and swam away.

The water grew suddenly lighter in colour and thicker. It might have been spilled cream. And all at once the fish came up: catfish, cod, bream, yellowbelly lined up fin to fin. Up river, down river, on both banks, thousands of fish of all sizes, every fish in the river, held their mouths out of the water and gulped air. We had never conceived of so many fish.

Where a clean creek ran into the river and cleared a wide V of deep water, the river showed its greatest prizes. Six Murray Cod circled head to tail, distant and safe from the men wielding gaffs on the river banks. They were the giants who will never be caught, fifty kilogrammes in weight, one and a third metres long, legends incarnate.

Celebration

The water grew browner and thinner. Gills could work again. All at once the fish were gone, the yabbies, the shrimps. The river was just a brown muddy stream in part flood. It acknowledged no secrets.

Another memory of the river was a simple thing. I was fishing. A water rat came out of the water near me and stood watching me. He dripped water. When a water rat climbs on to a part-submerged log with a freshwater mussel, he shakes the water off it vigorously before he opens it. He did not shake himself. Why should he? Water feels good to him. I wrote a poem about that water rat. Each sense has its own poem. Here is sight's.

Water Rat

Wet and yet not wet –
His slicked-down coat is impermeable.
Water is not in his soul
As in a fish's.
He sheds water like an oil-cloth
While he regards me

From a distance of no more than four feet,
Not with the panicky uncertainty
Of house-mouse or sewer-rat –
He stands nervously steadfast like a young parson
Knowing he can flick into another world in a moment
And be gone.

Why is rat?
Can a yellow bar on a long tail justify existence?
One Eclectus Parrot can colour a jungle.
Life did not come as wonderfully out of the hot mist
As that red bird out of the green.
How much river can rat colour?
No more than a veined stone.

You can't even fit him into a scheme:
Say 'Take away rat and the river will choke with mussels
Or dead fish putrefy the water'.
There's not enough of rat to matter.

Sight

The few opened shells on an exposed log
Are less than the falling river forgets in the mud
And yabbies scour all bones.

His mate comes and grasps him by the tail.
Rat twists backwards to join her.
Their wakes mingle and spread as they swim to mid-stream.
She takes his tail again.
They undulate like a long serpent.
They circle and roll and dive.
They break apart and he pursues her.
The river is agitated by their playing.
Concentric waves ring out to the water's edge.
The weeds are thus shaken.
Startled mayflies rise.
Their shadows, their images, flash in the water.

The rats are gone.
The last waves diffuse.
You don't have to justify existence.
Celebration is sufficient reason.

Our present farm joins a native forest. The boundary fence sharply divides land where European grains and domestic livestock thrive from land that will tolerate nothing that is not Australian. A hundred and fifty years ago the forest was open grassland. Squatters brought in sheep and cattle. The land reacted and drove them out with a wild growth of trees.

Where the rainfall seems insufficient, the soil too poor, plants grow in such profusion their roots intermingle and entangle. Cypress pine and eucalypts dominate the growth. Peaflowers, cassia, twenty-odd species of acacia support them with the nitrogen that bacteria build round their roots. In spring the grey-green forest glows yellow with their bloom, the distillation of a year's sun. Beneath them ground orchids, grasses, fan flowers, five corners, daisies, saltbush, geebungs, hundreds of plants mass in such interdependence their roots function almost as common roots. Supplejack, a small twisted tree, acknowledges its need for company. Its young growth is too pliant to support it, so it

Celebration

writhes about on the ground till it finds something to climb up, and it leans on its companion till its trunk hardens. Quandongs whose big fruits blaze red and yellow through the forest when they are ripe cannot grow unaided at all. Their young roots catch hold of other plants' roots with suction pads; their cells invade its cells; and, for a year or two, they mesh their lives with others as parasites until they learn to live alone.

I have spent a lifetime in wonder. I thought I had all the wonder I could contain. But the forest increased it. Within the last few weeks, after this book was well begun, I took out buckets of water early one morning and poured them over a Rock Fern to watch the effect. These plants are known as resurrection plants. Their recovery after drought is phenomenal.

I selected a fern that was growing on its own. There had been no rain for months. Some of its fronds were brown and dead, some still had a tinge of green, but they were shrivelled and so brittle they broke into dust at a touch. For a metre or so around it nothing seemed to be alive except a little hump of moss about half a centimetre high, six centimetres across. It felt dry but its yellow-green colour suggested life. For the rest there were cast pine needles, twigs, dead eucalyptus leaves.

I thoroughly wet the fern. I soaked the ground about it. I went back to look in twenty minutes. Wherever the water had run the ground was green. The fern had not changed. The hump of moss had simply grown into a light green plushy cushion with a pile one and a half centimetres high. But another moss had sprung from the dead and dotted the wet ground thickly. Scalloped-edged thalli, two centimetres long, one broad, lay flat on the ground like freshly dropped leaves.

I went to look again in the late afternoon. The morning moss had fruited and shrivelled once more. It was difficult to find any trace of it. A longer-lived moss had taken its place. It, too, lay flat on the ground with oval thalli in opposed pairs or in dark green spread-fingered fans. Next morning the fern had unrolled all those fronds showing a trace of green. The segments were fleshy and healthy. In a

Sight

week the dead fronds had broken off. New growth replaced them.

Amongst a host of trees individual trees assert themselves. A Kurrajong is a low-growing bushy tree. A specimen fifteen metres high is tall. In one of our timber strips a Kurrajong, forced up by big White Boxes all round it, has grown ninety centimetres in diameter and thirty metres tall. It is a king of Kurrajongs. We treasure it. A hundred years cannot replace it. Another Kurrajong germinated about fifty years ago in the top of a dead stump about four metres high. Now it is a good-sized tree. What should be its trunk is a thick cord of twisted roots that followed down the dust and termite debris in the hollow stump until they reached the ground. One sees them through ever-widening cracks. The dry stump is now no more than a casing, a split chrysalis the Kurrajong roots bulge through.

In another paddock one Native Apricot in its summer season hangs its pendulous branches with bitter, splitting, orange-pink fruit. At the house in November a Silky Oak spurts orange flames above the roof. Honeyeaters flock to the nectar, singing, chattering, or croaking according to species, feasting quickly, quarrelling often. And old planted White Cedars, one of the few seasonally deciduous trees in Australia, mass themselves in lilac each spring before they break into leaf. Delicately, for a month, the house floats in perfume. Banana Orchids grow on some of the cedars, planted there by birds. They look like bunches of rushes for most of the year, then in January they hang down heavy sprays of yellow-brown flowers splotched with red and darker brown.

Apart from its flowers, the aspect of the Australian bush is yellow grey-green. It is broken not by changes in tone but by the differing textures of hard leaves, soft leaves, needle leaves, phyllodes, by bark, by the open patches the sky shows through. In New Guinea I stood on the narrow spine of Shaggy Ridge, a mountain humped like the back of an angry boar, and I counted thirty-seven tones of green. It knows so much life, that country, death is inconsequential.

In its jungles I followed paths of green light. Once a Blue Birdwing Butterfly defied the green. I came on it resting on

Celebration

the ground, feeding on the droppings of a cassowary. Its heavy body pulsed. Sometimes it spread its wings. They shimmered, an eighteen-centimetre stretch of blue and black. I waited until it had finished feeding. I did not want to disturb it and lose it in the green.

Birds of Paradise screamed out of sight. They were trying to force their colours through the green. Goura Pigeons thrashed beside me. Sometimes they flew slowly down the path ahead and perched on a branch above it. Three kilogrammes of pale blue feathers and plump awkward flesh fearlessly let me approach. But no stillness could hold their topknots steady. Fine as cobweb, an exquisite lace of feathers shivered above their heads. These seemingly solid birds accentuated our fragility.

When Eastern Rosellas go to water, the reflections of their red breasts meet them as they dip their beaks. A row of these birds so stains the water one expects the colour to hold after they fly away. The male Superb Blue Wren feeds fussily with his five or six lively females. They cock their tails and hop and peck and chirp to keep in touch. The male hops with them but every now and again he becomes conscious of his beauty. He freezes in the sunlight. Momentarily he is an opal. Blues and blacks roll through him. He flashes. Then he goes on feeding.

When our first granddaughter was five months old, she learnt one morning to turn over. Immediately she rolled back again the other way, then, fully aware that she was doing something worth watching, she checked to see that we were all watching her before she turned over again.

I like an audience, too, little girl, for my words.

Taste

Top lips taste sweet, bottom lips acrid. The tracts between have their own flavours. I kissed her once in a Bathurst motel. It was hot early summer afternoon. We had travelled several hundred kilometres. We were naked and about to shower together. I kissed her again and extended the kisses. She was saltier than sea water all over – lips, cheeks, breasts, belly, buttocks, cunt. Her pubic hair glistened with droplets of heavy brine; Lot's wife in the dew. We could not stop kissing. Something had interrupted the last few days and we had not made love for a week. We laughed. Our sweaty bellies squelched together. We could not wait. We made love urgently and immediately. And much later had the long, slow, clean lovemaking we had planned. But sometimes it is good to do it quick and dirty.

A Trobiand Island girl, honey-skinned, runs out of the sea with water hanging in her crimped pubic hair. She places a piece of ripe fish between the lips of her vulva and shakes herself. 'Are you hungry?' she asks. 'Here is fish seasoned by the sea. Do not bite harder than you have to.'

The small amount of salt we use in cooking and at table is sea-salt out of the open-air evaporation pans at Whyalla in South Australia. Sometimes a hill of salt waits there for railway trucks to take it to the refining works. Tractors and harrows break it up in the pans. Bulldozers push it up to elevators that mound it ten metres high, twenty metres wide, and a kilometre long. When we get it, it is crusted with clay from the bottom of the pans, coated with wind-blown sand. We hose most of the dirt off a few lumps at a time, swirl them round in the water, dry them and crush them fine enough to feed through a hand grinder. There is a modern fad that such salt is healthier. It is not. But it tastes better.

The best salt is rock-salt from solidified ancient lakes. It comes in blocks speckled with granite, reddened by oxides of iron. None has been found in Australia, and what is

Celebration

imported is imported as animal food. So we do not risk eating it. One never knows what awful leaking containers a low-priced animal food might have been stored against. But until recent times in France, when even the best restaurants conditioned themselves to economies, if one wanted salt one asked the waiter for *la planche de sel,* and he brought to the table a solid little board and a wooden mallet to break up a red lump of rock-salt.

What sort of salt did François I put in the salt cellar Benvenuto Cellini made for him? Two solid gold figures, one male, one female, sit opposite one another and lean back with their legs interlaced. The naked male represents the sea, the naked woman the land. Around them and beneath them sport their gold animals. Waves are laid on the gold in blue and green enamels. The four winds blow. Dawn, day, twilight, night follow one another round the base. In one hand the man holds a hollow ship for salt. The woman holds a hollow temple for pepper. The cellar was not intended for passing. It sat heavily in the centre of the table on an oval of black ebony twenty centimetres long. Each of the main figures is ten centimetres high. Cellini gave the measurements in the strange old reckoning from the human body: two thirds of a cubit long, he said – two thirds of his forearm, one palm high.

The plastic bags of fine salt one sees on supermarket shelves, the cardboard packets of table salt, are refined of everything except convenience. They mate with cardboard cylinders of powdered pepper. Both pour easily into the nasty shakers designed for them, one with a small hole in the top for salt, one with rows of little holes for pepper dust.

Throughout the 1930s Cerebos brilliantly advertised the convenience of refined salt. They sold it in tin cylinders that emptied through a lift-up, push-down spout in the shape of a quarter-circle. *See how it runs* appeared on the tins, in newspaper advertisements, on huge hoardings beside railway lines and in every country town. And a man chased a cockerel that was running for its life. For when most chickens were caught, not bought, everyone knew the easiest way to catch them was to put a pinch of salt on the tail.

When we brought our last bag of salt from Whyalla, five of us waded at low tide on to the wide, sandy shallows of

Taste

Spencer Gulf. We carried buckets and home-made wire prongs, and in less than an hour we raked eighty big Blue-swimmer Crabs from their hides in bare sand, and speared them before they could swim sideways into surrounding weeds. The flesh of these crabs is fine-grained and delicate, the best of all. We carried them home, tipped them into a copper of cold water, threw in a lump of claypan salt, and brought them to the boil. We ate them hot. There were slices of lemon to squeeze on the meat, lumps of fresh wholemeal bread and butter and glasses of cold beer. We threw the shells into the empty buckets and realised that nowhere else could we have such a feast.

The coastal tribes of Papua New Guinea cook in sea-water. They fish in it, bathe in it, sail their boats in it. Sometimes they harvest the salt from evaporated rock pools and trade it up to a week's walk inland. But most of New Guinea's salt, a main article of trade among inland tribes, comes from a spring in the central highlands. Thousands of years ago a giant sow urinated in the limestone mountains. The outpouring flooded through underground cracks and began to seep from a hill near the collection of villages known as Wabag. The villagers tasted the spring water and found it so good they decided to harvest its essence and market it. So they dug a series of trenches about a metre deep where the spring would keep them full. Each family group dug the number of bays they had the numbers to operate. And for hundreds of years they have maintained them. Bays are bought and sold, leased, handed down in families.

This is how they get the salt. The men go into the mountains and chop down softwoods. They bark them and cut them into billets about forty-five centimetres long. Men and women carry the logs back and stack them in sheds thatched with pandanus for about a year until they are dry and as light as balsa. Several timbers are suitable but all have the same quality: they are exceptionally absorbent and they burn leaving little ash. Then each family fills its bays with these logs stood on end and seals them with densely-woven grass mats topped with about twenty centimetres of soil.

In three months' time when they are saturated, the women, conditioned to discomfort, lift the now heavy logs out of the bays and the men carry them back to the drying sheds.

Celebration

After more months in the stack the water evaporates leaving the salt behind. Then the men burn the logs under cover in day-long, night-long vigils. They parcel the salty white ash in banana leaves while it is warm, and strap it with tape made out of dried pandanus leaves. The neat parcels are waterproof and weigh about two and three-quarter kilogrammes. And the traders come in carrying live pigs on poles, cassowaries, stone axes, steel axes, pottery cooking pots, cowrie shells, Bird of Paradise plumes, rice, sago, sweet potatoes, cloth, tobacco, betel nut and the lime to bring up its flavour, now even Coca-Cola and tinned beef.

From settlement until a good third of the way through the twentieth century, the Australian rural worker, when he camped out, tried to live on black tea, damper and salt meat. Fresh meat everywhere was a careful assessment between the kill and rotten meat. Even in homes, the ice-chests of the cities, the hessian-sided drip safes of the country, and later, the big, charcoal-packed evaporative coolers could not give more than a day or two of extra fresh meat.

When I was a child most of the meat eaten in country homes was salt. We cured it in the universal container of those days, an emptied rectangular four-gallon kerosene tin with the top cut out and the rough edges hammered down smooth. A handle of soft 10-gauge fencing wire was looped through punched holes. We added two cupfuls, or two double handfuls, of coarse salt to twelve litres of water and boiled it over an open fire to dissolve the salt. If one had any doubt about the strength of the brine, one tried a fresh egg in it when it cooled. If the egg floated the brine was heavy enough. Then we packed in the cuts of lamb we could not eat in two days – both shoulders certainly, the rib pieces, one leg perhaps, some of the loin chops – brought the meat to the boil, and carried it to the meat room which often doubled as a laundry.

The tins became crusted black on the bottom, smoked grey and brown on the sides. With each killing the patina darkened. Two U-shaped pieces of stiff wire hung from a rafter above where the tin of meat stood in our laundry. These were sprung diagonally across the inside of the tin to stop any of the pieces of meat floating. Then a clean wheat bag was thrown over the top. Ten to fifteen millimetres of fat set on top of the brine and sealed it off.

Beef was dry salted. The cuts were rubbed with coarse salt, brown sugar and a little saltpetre, and stacked to drain. Each morning the meat was resalted, turned, and stacked in a different order. Bloody liquid ran from it. After about three weeks, the meat stopped weeping. It could then be hung up and would keep for weeks.

On an outstation in the Channel Country of far-western Queensland an Aboriginal stockman's wife gave us a piece of salt beef. It looked inedible. The surface was brick hard and blacker than the hand that took it out of an old chaff bag. 'It's good' she said with a huge smile. We thanked her. That night, camped a hundred kilometres away in a wilderness of wildflowers that is usually Sturt's Stony Desert, we almost threw the meat out. But we had been eating canned food for days and wondering that good food could become so unrecognisable and so unpleasant after being sealed in a tin. We had never tasted Channel Country beef. I cut off the hard crust. There was marbled red meat inside. We boiled it on a gas primus. The meat was delicious, tender and spiced with native herbs. The Channel Country is normally dry country. It runs a breeding cow to about two hundred hectares. But every several years Cooper's Creek comes down thirty kilometres wide and is distributed even farther by anabranches and shallow offshoots ending in blind lakes. For eight or nine months this great strip of naturally irrigated country becomes the finest fattening country in the world. The stations hurry all the stock they can buy on to the land. It will fatten five beasts to the hectare before the feed shrivels. The soil rebuilds itself in the next long dry. And when the flush comes again the grasses and herbs grow rich in minerals, rich in flavour.

Ways of cooking salt meat are limited. Until the 1950s eating was seldom an adventure in Australia. In the nineteenth century Chinese offered superb food and some European Australians discovered it, but most considered such food outlandish and unchristian. After Federation cosmopolitan Australia regressed to a dull and defensive outpost of Empire. Up to the beginning of World War II we sang

Celebration

Kipling's *Recessional* at school speech days. Thank God we groaned the words! It was embarrassed boasting:

> God of our fathers, known of old –
> Lord of our far-flung battle-line –
> Beneath whose awful Hand we hold
> Dominion over palm and pine ...

We felt no pity for 'the lesser breeds without the Law'. They sounded interesting.

A thriving Greek community that built up after World War I took over the country town cafés. Greek sold to Greek. Greek financed Greek. If a young man made enough money to get married, he went home by boat to find a Greek wife. And by serving food that was a parody of the worst Australian food, they prospered astoundingly. Slabs of steak fried ten minutes too long came to the table with one or two eggs on top, and surrounded by potato chips, mashed potato, mashed pumpkin, sliced lettuce, tomato, canned carrots, pickled beetroot. Thinly sliced white bread accompanied it. Bottles of tomato sauce and Worcestershire sauce sat on every table. And they were frequently emptied.

Sometimes I watched Greek proprietors sit down to their own meals at a back table. A waitress came from the kitchen with chunks of dark bread, blocks of white fetta or creamy broccio, black olives, grapes, broken lettuce leaves tossed in garlicky oil. Not eating much garlic then, I could smell it from several tables away. Now I am as seasoned as they were.

Edward Hallstrom saved country Australians from salt meat. In the 1940s he engaged a hefty offsider, loaded a truck with his Silent Knight refrigerators and drove round selling them. He would limp up to the door of every homestead in a district saying 'It won't make you much ice but it'll keep your meat'. And so it would, for three whole weeks if needed, especially if the refrigerator was used for nothing else. He soon had many trucks on the road. But the refrigerators were not silent. They were activated by two kerosene burners with wicks fifteen centimetres in diameter. Each night we filled the four-litre tank with kerosene and lit the burners. They roared like a forge for four hours, then went out with a puff of black smoke. The smell of burnt wick and kerosene pervaded sleep. For the rest of the night the coiled pipes behind the refrigerator gurgled, thumped, and trickled. The knight had noisy bowels.

Modern refrigerators seldom keep meat as well, often because they are not given a chance. Meat keeps best in dry air at 4.5°C. So those automatic defrosting models with water dripping on to exposed evaporation trays are too humid. Refrigerators set to chill a lot of soft drinks are too cold for meat. The drawers marked *Meat* or even *Meat Keeper* are designed to send meat bad quickly. Meat needs air circulating about it. It should be placed straight on the refrigerator shelves, not on plates, never in plastic bags.

As important as the refrigerator is the meat to be kept in it. Even when staying in cities we do not buy meat from supermarkets, we do not buy from the trays in butchers' windows. We inspect the trays and if the meat looks good we go into the shop, explain to the butcher which animal we want, what age, what cut. We ask to see the carcass. We ask him to cut our meat in one piece. Joan buys meat with all her faculties.

We carry sharp knives and a board with us and chop chops, slice steak and score pork as we need it. Meat tastes better that way. We enjoy meat. Flesh is the foundation of a meal. The rest is garnish. The flesh determines the meal: the wine, the sauce, the garnishes. It governs the soup or the entrée, influences the pudding.

We kill our own meat – we select it alive. We like our lamb twelve to fourteen weeks old, about thirty-five kilogrammes in weight. It is still sucking its mother but it has eaten enough pasture to flavour it. It is plump. Its wool with the curly lamb tip has a greasy sheen. We catch it in the late afternoon by a hind leg, lift it with both hands under the brisket. A careless grab at the wool on the sides could turn four of the best chops into bruised pulp. How do we kill it?

There is a nasty breach between the living lamb and the good flesh. I can look at the lamb when it is alive dispassionately. I can value it as food. For the brief period of the kill it is a creature in agony. I lie it on its side, kneel at its back, pin its loin with my right knee, cup its chin in my left hand and stretch its head back. Then I take a sharp knife in

Celebration

my right hand, steel myself, and slash its throat crosswise to the bone. Blood gushes from the jugular, spurts a metre from an artery. Air rasps in the severed windpipe. I move my right knee nearer the shoulder and force the head right back till the neck breaks. Then I cut the spinal cord between the severed vertebrae.

I stand away. Blood gurgles. The lungs suck air in slow, noisy gasps. The legs kick spasmodically, then violently. The lamb makes a last rush to catch up with life. And suddenly it is meat. I knife the skin off the legs and shoulders and leave it dangling, open up the neck, skin the face, keeping the ears on so the registered mark proves one has not killed a neighbour's lamb, punch the tough skin off the brisket with the handle of the knife (the men who do this job in abattoirs use their clenched fists, and their knuckles are calloused and distorted), lift the skin off the belly by punching my fist from brisket to crutch, slit the lifted belly skin with the knife, and hang the lamb up by that coat-hanger-shaped bar known as a gambrel with a hook on each end and an eye in the middle where the winch-rope ties on. Then I punch all the skin off, slit open the belly and remove the innards.

Our young children waited for them to drop with a squelch on the ground. One picked up the anus that I had cut out in a neat circle while still attached to the rectum and began to pull. The other disentangled the coiled intestines and fed them out carefully, calling instructions. 'Don't pull too hard, you'll break it! Will this lamb break the record? How long is its guts? Don't pull so hard! Watch that bit of roly-poly, it'll tear it!' And when the astonishing length was stretched to its utmost and a new peg put in to mark the end, the thin line became a telephone line. 'It's won! It's won!' was shouted up the anus to the ear nearly touching the paunch, or 'Aw! It's just a no-good short guts.'

Some old butchers, expert skinners and proud of their meat, used to incise rosettes and trailing stems and leaves on each side of the carcasses. Such carving would get lost in the little cuts and tears of my inexpert skinning. I am glad to hide the lamb in the white bag that keeps the early morning blowflies off and leave it overnight to set. Meat cut hot contracts into tough awkward shapes.

Chinese do not skin sheep. When Chinese gold-seekers dodging the Victorian poll-tax marched across South Australia in thousands they bought sheep from landholders on the way to the diggings. The bigoted graziers of the 1850s laughed to see the Chinese scalding and plucking the wool off the sheep they killed. 'The ignorant heathens' they said, 'they don't know how to skin a sheep.' And the Chinese, as bigoted as the landholders, declared that nobody but a red-faced barbarian would discard the skin, such an essential part of the flesh.

What parts of the lamb do we discard? I thought little until I read old French recipes. Australians are careless with meat. There is so much of it, most of it has to be exported. Our sheep, our cattle, even our wild rabbits could supply a population hundreds of times its present size. In the few years of euphoria between the end of the depression and the beginning of World War II country town butchers threw away forequarters of beef. Only the hindquarter was saleable. It responded better to careless cooking.

A hundred years before when Sydney butchers threw their offal into Sydney harbour, scroungers rowed out and collected the blown-up paunches and intestines as they floated, emptied them, washed them roughly in the seawater, picked up any floating hearts and lungs and sold them all to those so poor the butchers scorned to serve them.

I throw away the lambs' lungs; we cook the dark tough hearts for the dogs, well aware that the Scots mince both along with the liver which we do eat, mix them with oatmeal and suet and seasonings, stuff all of it into the cleaned stomach, and boil it as haggis. I like malt whisky straight. It is the essence of Scotland. But I do not like haggis. It tastes like peat.

I throw away the head after splitting it for the brains and cutting out the tongue. There is little enough flesh on it. It takes a long time to clean. The French bone the head, and stuff it and serve it with a wine and egg sauce, or else they cook it slowly with vegetables, and serve it with a sauce of its own brains.

A butcher in Marrickville, Sydney, where I lived when going to high school in the 1930s, had good winter sales of sheep's heads for making soup. One of his apprentices in a

Celebration

striped blue apron stood beside a meat block in a corner and cleaned and split heads for an hour or two at a time. All about him on the sawdust floor crawled the big, cream, lively maggots of bot-flies that invade the antra and nasal passages. None of his customers worried. They were aware then of the origins of meat and of the blemishes that go with origins. A modern housewife buying her sliced meat from plastic-covered trays in supermarkets does not see animals as she buys it. Its origins would repulse her. And one wonders at her reaction if she saw maggots three centimetres long wriggling beneath the tables of meat.

From that same butcher we bought pigs' cheeks, a strangely evasive term for those days. The cheek was attached to a half head. When cooked and laid out for carving on a big oval dish, the milky blue eyes stared unblinkingly through a fringe of lashes, the snout wrinkled. The cheek slices were delicious, so was the tongue. But I always feared, at the first touch of the carving knife, the flesh might waver and turn into the head of John the Baptist. Now we make brawn with the fleshy heads of the pigs we kill. The actual head seems too close to origins, especially when we have talked to it as it grew, pulled its ears, fed it and watched it eating.

Our pigs' trotters go into brawn with the head. I throw away the lambs' legs. The French clean them, split them in half lengthways, spread one half with forcemeat, sandwich the other on top of it, wrap them tightly in pig's caul which is a thin, clear, stomach membrane with globules of fat through it, fry them and serve them with a truffle and Madeira sauce. A good cook can turn waste into wonder if he must.

The best of the lamb is best cooked simply, but not unimaginatively. One remembers flavours. One builds them together like words for the best effect. Grill chops on a preheated griller till they are bubbly outside and pink inside and serve with a sauce of tomato, onion and parsley. Potatoes cooked in their jackets in the oven, split, buttered and peppered, go with them, and beans lifted from the open boiling pot while they are still crisp. All the flavours complement, textures compensate.

I called one morning to see a neighbour. His wife, an English girl, was about to cook breakfast. She had cold

Taste

lumps of lamb's liver in a pan with cold lumps of mutton fat. She was about to put it on the stove. 'Can you cook?' she asked. We slice liver wafer thin, dip it in egg, coat it with breadcrumbs, drop it into bubbling butter, cook it till the egg and breadcrumbs set on top, throw in a cup of red wine, wait till it boils, serve it. And liver is a different meat.

A leg of lamb can be rubbed with garlic, sprigged with rosemary, baked in claret, or else braised slowly in cream with a bay leaf, lemon juice, curry powder. A shoulder can be boned, stuffed with onion, breadcrumbs, parsley, and dried apricots soaked in milk, rolled and baked. That is an unexpected matching of flavours and one that is right. Good cooks, good poets astonish. They make things their own and present them new.

Some flesh, some fruits, enhance one another: duck and green olives, chicken and lemon, pheasant and raspberry, Murray Cod and white grapes, scallops and pears, beef and mushrooms, ham and brown figs – black figs are too scented – pork chops and prunes. Pork is an opulent meat. Spread prunes between two chops, tie them together, put them in a casserole with onions and a full stock, add cabbage before cooking is finished, and simple things blend themselves into a rich dish.

Pigs are fed like poultry. They are not left to graze like cattle and sheep. Since what I eat I am, they do not select their own flesh. It is spread on them by rations designed for profit, not flavour. And since so many animals are now yarded and fed, there is a blurring of taste in meat. Cattle, pigs, chickens, ducks, pheasants, lambs, domestic rabbits have a common background flavour.

Italian prosciutto is first spiced on the pig by the aromatic herbs it is fed. Rouen ducklings are smothered so that no part of the built-in flavour runs out with the blood. The flesh is dark red and has to be cooked soon after the bird is killed. Blood is an ideal medium for bacteria and unbled meat goes bad quickly. Women use little augers and tubes thrust down the necks of the monstrous Strasbourg geese to wind flavour into the livers as they grow pale and huge for *paté de foie gras*. Ducklings for the great restaurants of Beijing that seat thousands of diners at a time are force-fed and flavoured on farms in hundreds of thousands. The

Celebration

attendants of the heifers fattened in Japanese pens as Kobe beef, the world's most expensive meat, groom their charges each morning and tease their coats with straw whisks. In the evening they reward them for a good day's eating with bottles of beer.

Letting the stock out of Australian yards would not alter the flavour much. Most paddock feed is also monotonous: sown single crops or pastures of two or three species. Any special flavour is likely to be nasty. Lucerne, a universal pasture, exaggerates the slight woolly flavour of sheep. When wild turnip grew prolifically in the north-west of New South Wales one year, a weed with a persistent, sickening, bitter taste, the Gunnedah abattoirs employed a man to smell the breath of all sheep and cattle sent for slaughter. Those with the turnip taint had to be fed in yards for a week or so till they smelt clean.

We buy the pigs we kill to eat when they are weaned at six weeks of age and we feed them a ration of mixed grains, protein supplements and minerals. We let them out to graze every few days. It gives them the chance to make some selection of their own flavour. Anyway, they enjoy it. They snort and jump and chase one another about and grab greedy mouthfuls of grass and roots and dirt.

It is harder to kill a pig than a lamb, not only because more preparation is needed, but because pigs are more intelligent and have more character than lambs. We have fed them for two months. We know them. They squeal when it is feed time. We call out to let them know we are coming. After their run in the paddock we call and they come back. I scold one if it makes a playful grab at my boots as I walk through the pen. Another likes to be stroked on the back, one on the nose.

First pig has reached fifty kilogrammes – killing weight. We admire her as flesh. We'll roast that shoulder, cut the other with the belly into a long hand for Chinese cooking. That's a beautiful leg. Poor pig looks doubtful. She is aware of the difference in attitude. We hang the small block and tackle on a leaning limb of the shade tree next to the yard. We prop a 200-litre drum on bricks, fill it with water, and build a fire under it. I sharpen knives, find the old bread saws we use as scrapers. We set up a plank table to scrape her on.

I get a small bucket of feed, make happy feeding time noises, tip it into the trough. If first pig is engrossed in eating she will be easier to catch. All six pigs are hungry. They missed the morning feed. It is less messy to butcher an animal with an empty paunch. None of them come. They sulk in a corner. I climb into the pen with the light chain we use to hang the pigs up. I catch first pig by a hind leg. Her mouth opens and squeal comes out in a continuous flow. I slip the chain above her knuckle, hold it in place, catch her other leg in my other hand, and steer her on her front legs out of the pen to the gallows tree. Pig squeals harder. She can draw breath and squeal at the same time. I hook the chain to the rope on the block and tackle, someone hauls on the other end. Pig lifts off the ground. She hangs upside down with her neck level with my waist. I take a very sharp, pointed knife and open her thick skin downwards from brisket to throat. Pig squeals harder. Then I turn the knife, plunge it to the bone, and draw it upwards. A pig's neck is thick, the blood vessels deep. It is a very quick movement but it seems to take minutes. Three centimetres are opened fifteen centimetres deep – no blood. Seven centimetres are open, ten, a hideous wound. All one can hear is squealing pig. The knife point touches the brisket. I lift it. And blood pours out as though a bag has burst. European women hold out basins to catch it and they make blood puddings to a recipe handed down twenty-nine centuries from the still-famous pork butchers of Tyre. We waste it. It spreads on the ground.

The flow of blood, the flow of squeals stop together. Pig is meat. The water has reached 62°C. We lower the carcass in, move it about for a couple of minutes, then lift it out on to the scraping table. The hair slips off with the paper-thin top skin and the carcass is firm, white, smooth and rounded. A layer of fat about a centimetre deep underlies the thick skin that bubbles into a crisp, aromatic crust, the crackle, on every slice of roast pork.

We sometimes salt cure a shoulder of pork. We no longer make ham and bacon. The modern methods are better than

Celebration

the old – the meat is softer and less salty. But we travel two hundred kilometres to buy it from a man who cures it as we like it. I enjoyed the smoking of ham and bacon. A low tunnel about one and a half metres long carried the smoke of hardwood sawdust – and cooled it on the way – to a covered 4550-litre iron tank where the meat was hung. We tended the fire night and day for eighty hours. And the meat that went in as reddish salt pork bloomed shiny and amber as ham and bacon. We covered the ham in a flour crust for baking. Now we wrap it in aluminium foil. We cut the bacon in eight-millimetre thick slices. We still do. If we cannot buy bacon in the piece we do without it. Good eating is eating when the best is available.

There are superstitions about food. Pigs' brains will send you mad. Pigs' livers are poisonous. There are a lot of recipes for pigs' brains and livers. Childhood cautions destroyed my appetite for them. The water that eggs are boiled in will give you warts. Long green cucumbers will give you stomach ache unless you extract the poison. You cut the end off and rub the cut edges together. Do you see all that froth coming out? That's the poison.

But no one told Douglas Mawson, starving in Antarctica, that the livers of Husky dogs are poisonous. He and his companion sacrificed their sled dogs, ate the livers as the most nourishing food. They contain more vitamin A than the human body can tolerate. Mawson lost the soles of his feet, skin sloughed from his legs and arms. His companion, Xavier Mertz, died. Mawson dragged himself to safety.

The Chinese call dog 'the fragrant flesh'. 'Young black dogs are best to eat,' a Chinese from Guangdong Province told me, 'old yellow cats. Eat dog in Guangzhou, not in Beijing. We cook it better.' It would be an experience to try Dragon's Duel Tiger. Wildcat and snake oppose one another across the sauce they were cooked in.

In the 1940s I watched a country abattoir at work in Wingham, New South Wales. The kill for the day was pigs and calves. A man with a double-headed sledge-hammer stepped into a pen of thirty week-old calves. He swung his hammer to the left; hit a calf between the eyes; it dropped. He swung to the right; another dropped. The awful pendulum never faltered. Another man worked to its rhythm, cutting throats as the calves dropped. Five full pens in a line awaited them. The dead were hooked to chains on a moving line.

In another part of the works pigs were hoisted alive on a moving chain. Twenty pigs of all sizes hung by their hind legs and squealed. They passed through a U-shaped opening in the round, cement-walled bleeding tank. The slaughterman stuck each pig as it passed. He worked in gumboots and shorts. Sometimes a charge of blood hit him in the stomach. He stood six centimetres deep in blood. It matted his hair, dripped from his elbows, soaked his shorts. The noise was horrific. Each stuck pig was carried on a slow circuit of the tank while it finished bleeding and squealing, then it passed out to the steamy scalding troughs. About six pigs at a time were tossed about by rubber arms, then passed between revolving brushes that stripped the hair off.

I was astonished to find the experience distressed me. There was more blood than I could cope with, more meat than I could ever eat, more death rattles than I ever expected to hear. Every living thing I was to eat for the rest of my life and more protested to me at once. Still, does a cut lettuce scream silently, or a cucumber vine tremble at my touch?

A man in Papua New Guinea cries his heart out as he strangles the cassowary he has reared from a chicken. It is a test of manhood as well as the preliminary to a feast. If a cassowary uncoils its neck and struggles to its feet alive, its owner is disgraced. Pig-killing is a joyous occasion. Villages join together. Visiting men come in singing, shouting, and carrying poles in pairs with black pigs, striped pigs dangling from them. Women and children lead the quieter pigs by liana canes tied to their forelegs. When all the guests have arrived, when the pigs are staked in lines, someone shouts the word and the men rush to the pigs with heavy clubs. One, two, three, four, five blows it takes between the ears to kill some of them. The cooking fires are ready; they were lit the day before. The air shimmers above long trenches lined with glowing stones and big red coals. The scattered surface fires used for singeing the hair off flare brightly. The men cut up the meat. They turn the chunks over, admire them. Girls grab the intestines and run laughing into the river to strip them clean. Offal is a delicacy. The older

Celebration

women and some of the men singe the cuts of meat, wrap them in banana leaves and lay them in a cooking trench. When all the stones and coals are covered, they throw in about twenty centimetres of soil and leave the meat to cook slowly for four hours.

On the first day the meat is rich and gamy, the wild boar that has been treasured for centuries. But the blood and the climate sends the meat bad quickly, and the people, starved of protein for most of the year, overestimate what they can eat. None of the flesh must be thrown away. That would prejudice all future feasts. The usual end is the gorging of tainted meat.

There is irregular feasting on the Ramu River when it unwinds itself from its maze of channels through a sunken bed two kilometres wide, and charges downstream as one huge river. Drowned animals come down with it: cassowaries, wallabies, pigs, cuscuses, big rats, even, now, sheep and cattle. Word of the flood races ahead of it. Tribes line the banks. Men with poles, men in canoes, women and children gather the chance harvest. There is such a general shortage of protein in the inland of Papua-New Guinea all flesh is welcome.

One mountain tribe exposes its dead on open tree platforms and sets oval wooden trays under them to catch mature maggots as they drop to ground. They clean them in moss and eat them. After several quick deaths the health of the tribe picks up. South Australians fishing for the little, good-eating Tommy Ruffs harvest their bait in much the same way. They clean the maggots that drop off a dead fowl or rabbit in bran, and pack them in covered cartons. When Tommy Ruffs come on the bite on a dark night, few of the fishermen lined up on the jetties can talk. They put up to four maggots at once on their little hooks, and they hold the next two or three baits conveniently ready in their mouths.

'If you want to work hard, Eric, you've got to have a good breakfast – thirteen eggs and a pound and a half of steak.' The man who gave me that advice over thirty years ago was two metres tall. He would have been even taller but a cranky working bullock had gored him in the neck when he was a youth and his bent spine cost him several centimetres. He was a giant of a man, and carried no unnecessary fat. Once when we were gravelling a stretch of boggy road – the only way to improve secondary country roads in those days was to do it oneself – four of us who could work hard shovelled the load off one side of a truck, he unloaded the other and finished before we did. His family's garden bore witness to their egg eating. They used egg shells as a mulch. From garden fence to walls of the house on all four sides, over all the big vegetable garden, there was a mottled brown and white layer of broken shells four centimetres deep.

When labour laws began to upset the comfortable authority of station owners and managers, one law caused a change in the homestead rations. The government pronounced that the meat killed for the men had to be of the same quality as the meat killed for the homestead. It was practice to kill lamb for the boss, old wethers for the men. Who could afford to feed station hands lamb? It would be unheard of extravagance. After the law, for a few months anyway, station owners and their families chewed their way through old wether.

Six-year-old Welsh mutton, ewe or wether, is a different meat, fine-grained and tender with a flavour no lamb has developed. The Australian merino is dark and coarse, and neither feeding nor cooking can improve it. Even its shape hanging up as a carcass is unattractive. Its hind legs form a long, narrow V. A good fat lamb hangs from a wide, short-sided U.

Each year on sheep farm or cattle station there are musters for marking, the rite that turns ram lambs into wethers, bull calves into steers. When stations ran fifty thousand sheep and more, many hands came together for lamb marking. It was common to mark four thousand a day. Up to six catchers worked together. And the operators with the knives scorned the use of mechanical grips. They cut off the tips of the scrotums, squeezed the testicles out, bent down and gripped them in their teeth, the most adept took both at once, drew back their heads till the long cords broke, and dropped the testicles into a bucket. None of the hands had brought any more for lunch than bread and tea. They picked the fattest of the bloodshot, creamy ovals out

Celebration

of the buckets and fried them over an open fire. Northern Territory stockmen on lonely mustering camps, Aboriginal and white, grill the big testicles of the bull calves they throw, brand and cut.

In Arabian countries lamb carcasses hang in Muslim butcher-shops with their bared testicles dangling to prove the meat is the lean male lamb fit for the faithful. As *animelles*, testicles are still regarded as delicacies in France, Spain and Italy: sliced, marinaded, fried in butter.

The control we have of the lives of animals sometimes disturbs me. I do not enjoy playing god, I would rather enjoy what the gods have made. 'He used to embarrass the women something awful' a farmer told me. 'You should've seen some of the contortions he got up to. Nearly turned hisself inside out.' His dog, bored with hours on the chain, had learnt to masturbate. He would lie on his side and lick his penis till the long thin prong, supported most unusually by a bone, extended. Then he jerked his hindquarters and slipped it across his tongue till the little knobs at the base of the bone came out of the prepuce and swelled into pronounced dumb-bells, the lock that would hold him joined to a bitch for twenty minutes. He sprang to his feet, humped his back, and scraped his penis against his chest. Each time the end protruded between his front legs, he licked it. He lay on his back, lifted his hind legs, and worked it against his belly. He bent his head down, he rolled into a hoop, and licked and jerked. The distance he could shoot the rather liquid ejaculate was a marvel to see.

'He got worse and worse. The missus was always complaining. So I stuck his head in a bag and I cut him. That was on a Monday. He did it once more on Wednesday. Then he was no good no more.' So the dog lies lazy in the dust. And the women do not blush at him.

Cockerels used to be turned into plump, smooth-skinned capons by a deep and awkward operation to extract the testicles that lie in recesses in the shelly bone that frames the back. No one in Australia would wait for capons to grow now or would pay for them when they did. The modern meat-chicken is a miracle of breeding. Prime chickens are ready in weeks instead of months. Most of the millions sold are wasted as nasty frozen chickens. Even those one buys

Taste

fresh are bland imitations of what they might be. We buy them as day-olds and feed them prepared rations as well as letting them out to select plants and insects to build their flavour. We begin eating them as poussins at four and a half weeks, one chicken per serving, and fit them as they grow into a sequence of recipes until one chicken serves six. They must all be eaten before fourteen weeks when they bloat into caricatures of plump chickens, breasts as wide as turkeys', and too grossly fat to eat.

These chickens seem to be designed rather than bred. A computer decided how fast they should grow for how much feed. It specified they should have two legs but it did not specify that legs were for walking on. Compressed in tiers of cages, no one notices whether they walk or not. When we turn them on to the ground as day-olds, they move as dubiously as if they had been thrown into water. They remain awkward. Their breasts are so wide they seem to be front heavy, and even though their legs are massive, they walk jerkily as though they might topple forward. They are designed to be eaten at nine weeks. If kept till older, some collapse at the knees and hobble along on their shanks.

Sometimes we set a few batches of crossbred game eggs so we can admire our chickens as individuals instead of as mass-produced marvels. They are ready at seven months, not seven weeks. They are as gay as pheasants and graceful – they move like fencers. And they are superb eating, too. But some are so beautiful it is difficult to kill them. One holds them with neck outstretched on the chopping block and brings down the axe. Wings flutter. Colours streak the air. I have beheaded a butterfly.

Some Middle Eastern markets display chickens plucked and alive. Fish dying tediously in the Hong Kong markets are split open so their beating hearts demonstrate freshness. With careless practicality Chinese ringbarkers in outback New South Wales tacked their ducks' webbed feet to the wooden floors of their sleeping huts. They put a dish of water and a dish of feed in front of each duck. It saved the expense of building pens, and there was no fear of ducks escaping while they were away at work.

The pheasants one eats now in Australian restaurants taste little different to chicken. They are fed much the same

Celebration

diet. Pheasants tasted more like pheasants when protein was supplied by mealworms, maggots and termites rather than vegetable proteins. Wild pheasant has a distinctive gamy flavour that is accentuated if the bird is hung for a day or two unplucked and undrawn. But any undrawn game has to be hung warily in Australia. If the temperature exceeds 16°C intestines and paunches puff up and burst, and the flesh turns putrid.

In England too many dishes taste as though the flavour got lost in a fog. But some of the game tastes as though it drowned in a sewer. There is an alarming liking for high meat. Woodcock, a bird so good to eat fresh one old French writer said it 'Sharpens the discernment of wine', is hung for six weeks till it stinks. Hare, a good rich meat when fresh, is hung till the hair slips from the skin, even till the body drops from the leg it is hung by. Apart from the taste, it is dangerous meat. There is risk of salmonella poisoning, or worse, botulism.

The giblets of chickens and ducks make good soup stock. The livers are not included in the giblets. They make exquisite paté and bitter soup. Europeans make other good dishes of giblets but most Australians cannot cope with identifiable flesh. They look at chicken legs on a plate as though they might leap off it and run across the table. Once in Papua-New Guinea I shot three wild ducks for the native lad who carried my rifle. He took them home proudly to his parents in the village. Next morning he offered me the six eyes cupped in his palm. I chewed two, then closed his hand over the others. He would never have tasted them. Children are given no delicacies. 'You are doing a man's job. You eat them.' I found them tasteless but obviously they did not disappoint him. No eyes ever tasted better. On Bougainville I lifted the lid of a big pot boiling on an open fire. World War II had ended two days before. We had just overrun a gun post whose occupants did not know the war had ended. In the pot a few grains of rice bounced through the fingers of two human hands. The starving Japanese soldiers had not murdered for them. Their emaciated owner lay dead a few metres away with no other marks of violence on him.

Years ago I wrote a poem about a good chicken dish. I still enjoy the dish, I still enjoy the poem. It is fooling with words, the essence of the most serious poem. The turkey, an American Bronzewing, is notable more for size than flavour. My father bred them for the English market. At seven months they weighed eighteen kilogrammes, as big as lambs.

Dinner

> Oh, a fine fat turkey gobbler –
> I stoved him with chestknots
> And breasted him with truffles
> And he roosted in the baking three hours.
>
> Then I did not care to speak.
> With savage knife and gruesome fork
> Wizard-like, mysteriously,
> I changed that turkey into me.
>
> But oven butter was a chicken
> Cajoled in wine and onion sauce
> And I a sculptor gleefully
> Carved that chicken into me.

It is stock that makes soup and if soup at the time of writing is out of fashion, perhaps it is because so many recipes begin 'Dissolve two large chicken cubes' or 'beef cubes'. Winter and summer soup is good, and bones and flesh are its foundation. Vegetables are vital in the stock but it is the chicken carcasses and the giblets that give it body, the fish heads and backbones left after filleting, the dark muscle of beef shins and the big bones broken to expose the marrow (and perhaps a calf's foot added), the gristly meat from lamb shanks and the broken bones. As a supplement, one that makes the good supreme, add the tablespoon or two of jellied juices from baking pans. One need not even label them in the refrigerator. Fat floats to the top as it cools and seals each little container. And it is obvious whether it is fish fat, beef fat, chicken fat, or mutton fat, for the colour and consistency are different.

So what soups does good stock make? Cold avocado soup, cold cucumber soup enrich a twenty-year-old Hunter

Celebration

River semillon as much as scallops in cream. Two Chinese soups match the best of French soups: chicken and sweet corn, and kidney and mushroom, provided it is made with fresh mushrooms. The different flavour of Chinese dried mushrooms, good as they are, fits only Chinese cooking. There are thick celery and potato soup, and broccoli soup, and fresh green pea soup – green and delicious – and yellow pumpkin soup that varies with the pumpkin from thick to thin and changes flavour from deep to delicate according to whether beef stock or chicken stock is used. We add a blob of thick cream to each bowl of pumpkin soup. Used to our own farm cream we once served this soup at a dinner party in Adelaide. We bought the cream in a cardboard box, all that was available, and never thought of it being thickened with gelatine. Instead of melting and spreading in a bright star, it congealed and bobbed as a dull little dumpling. But the soup still tasted good.

French onion soup has warmed winters all round the world for centuries. Crisp squares of bread float on top of it spilling sharp, grated Parmesan cheese over their edges. This hard golden-yellow cheese takes four years to mature, then keeps for twenty. The cheesemakers of Lombardy tap the big balls with hammers as they ripen, and if they detect a diseased soft patch, they cut it out like a cancer, and cauterise the wound with red-hot irons.

Bread is no longer the staff of life, though as I write this chapter the Labor Government of New South Wales controls the price of bread and gives it a value as a staple food it lost years ago. Good bread tastes good but it is hard to find. I like chunks of bread with soup or to mop up sauces, and thin buttered slices with prawns and pepper and lemon juice, and thick buttered toast in the morning. At the lively Victoria Market in Melbourne we bought a loaf of Kosher bread – dense, heavy, black, made of coarsely-ground rye, molasses and sour cream kneaded together with Yiddish blessings. It went superbly with a coarse beef terrine, a couple of radishes, a few slices of tomato, and a green salad tossed in oil and garlic, with a dab of yoghurt to pick up the sour flavour again. Housewives going home from supermarkets with packets of thin, white slices of congealed latex would take one bite of such bread and spit in astonishment. Their bread does not taste!

Mostly we buy our bread many loaves at a time wherever we can find unsliced wholemeal wheaten bread that tastes as though it is coloured by the flour, not by brown dye, and that has whole yellow grains to crunch on scattered through it. Then we freeze it at -15°C, a temperature that keeps it without petrifying it. When bread is wanted, sprinkle it with water and put it in the oven. Loaves months old taste like freshly-baked bread. It is one of the few foods that can be frozen without spoiling the texture.

So in country towns and several cities there are remembered bakers. There are many places we go to buy one outstanding product. Usually we never buy them elsewhere, and sometimes we go a year or two without, though we do travel up to a hundred kilometres out of our way to go past a special supplier. We buy green asparagus at Largs where it is packed in an old church hall that overlooks the silty Hunter River flood plain where it is grown. And in many kilogrammes of this notoriously stringy vegetable we have not found a string. Avocados come from Alstonville out of Lismore on the North Coast of New South Wales where a group of handicapped workers under superb management produce outstanding tropical fruit; fish from the lively Sydney Fish Market or the Fishermen's Cooperative at Nelsons Bay. A fisherman at Hobart in Tasmania sells his catch live from cages tied to the jetty where he moors his launch. And there are no finer crayfish than those sold from the South Australian Fishermen's Cooperative at Robe.

At Noarlunga out of Adelaide, where I fished for bream at night using the hairy-legged crabs one digs there for bait, a backyard grower produces that seldom seen vegetable, witloof. He grows it in raised beds covered with corrugated iron, flat iron, hessian, canvas, old sheets of masonite – anything he can find to shield it from the sun and blanch it. It is a white vegetable of little nutritive value but it has the flavour of exquisitely delicate celery.

We buy fat oysters in the shell from a farmer on a long, lovely, narrow arm of Port Stephens. In all but the hottest weather oysters keep for days in a shady, airy room, and they can be safely carried long distances. It is good, four

Celebration

hundred kilometres from the sea, washing and opening oysters that have brought the smell of the sea with them, and even better eating them knowing there is no better shellfish. I never order oysters at a restaurant. A chef likes to present his cooking and oysters are better plain. Nothing but lemon juice and a grind of pepper can improve them. One is even uncertain how quickly the tearing open of the shell kills them. They seem to flinch from the lemon juice. Perhaps one swallows them alive. It would be disconcerting if they moaned. Older Chinese knew a dish called Drunken Shrimps. A covered bowl of live shrimps was placed in the centre of the table. Each guest lifted the lid cautiously, reached out with his chopsticks and made a quick, deft catch, dunked the shrimp in the bowl of rice wine set before him, then ate it. Polluted streams put the dish out of favour. Now by Chinese law shrimps must be cooked.

I remember superb oysters at Yamba on the North Coast of New South Wales twenty years ago, and a strawberry farm a few kilometres out of town. One need not travel far anywhere for good strawberries but they are better off the farm than out of the shop. The extra few days on the plant lifts the flavour. Each time we bought strawberries at Yamba, we travelled a few kilometres farther to a dairy farm at the head of a creek, and bought fresh cream to go with them. At that time traditional dairyfarmers still owned the land. Some families had been there two or three generations. Like their animals they showed the deficiencies of the soil: they were small, light-boned, bow-legged, pale. Especially in the high mountain valleys, there were pockets of in-bred people. One or two members of a family were kept out of the way of visitors.

We bought our cream from a pleasant, tall Scottish woman with a good-looking daughter. They seemed to have none of the characteristics of North Coast people. One day we arrived later than usual. The girl's brother was bringing in the cows for the evening milking. We saw him pass between two sheds. His face was vacant, he shuffled, his hands turned outwards at an odd angle.

The clotted cream of Devon and Cornwall is made by standing fresh milk in a wide-mouthed earthenware bowl with sloping sides for twelve hours in their cool summer or

Taste

twenty-four hours in their cold winter. Then the bowl is put on the stove and heated slowly till the cream that has risen to the top shows the bottom of the pan as a disc concentric with the rim of the bowl. Then it is lifted from the heat as carefully as an old bottle of wine is lifted from the cellar and stood in a cool place for another twelve hours. The crust of cream is taken off with a perforated spoon or slice. It is fifteen or eighteen millimetres deep, yellowish, too thick to pour, with firmer lumps through it.

The ultimate sauce for strawberries is cream. No chef can equal it. It is good for other fruit, too, and it reinforces so many meat sauces. Cream is the finest product of the soil, an extract of its riches. It was not legal for that dairyfarmer to sell us cream. No one in Australia legally sells cream worth eating. What is sold in cartons tastes like poor imitation. Even our milk, pasteurised, infused with waxed cardboard, tastes like artificial milk. And most of it is also homogenised, the fat droplets are emulsified through it so that whoever pushes up the awkward spout of a container to get milk has not firstly to pour off a thin layer of thin cream, too thick for tea, too thin for sauce, the right consistency, but not the right flavour, for coffee. To get good cream one must milk one's own cow.

The self-sufficient islanders of Jersey and Guernsey in the English Channel developed their own breeds of cattle. The Jersey is a light and lively little cow, and produces a smooth, white, waxy cream good for butter-making. The Guernsey is bigger and quieter, an easy cow, with thick yellow cream of remarkable flavour. The Australian Illawarra Shorthorn produces good cream, too. I like best the cream that rises to the top of bowls put in the refrigerator. It is clotted cream, too. One gets less cream than by heating the milk as they do in Devon but it is sweeter cream without the slightly sharp tang of heated milk through it.

To get the most cream one must separate it by machine. I use an old hand separator Joan bought years ago at a sale. One pours fresh frothy milk in a big stainless steel bowl at the top, puts an empty bucket under the skim milk spout, a bowl under the cream spout, and turns a handle evenly and deliberately until the handle is turning at sixty revolutions a minute, and the machine is humming the right note. When the separator

Celebration

was new thirty or forty years ago, it had a governed hammer in the drive-shaft that struck a bell when the speed was right, so each morning the separator sang to the accompaniment of bells. Now when the buzz sounds right I turn the handle that lets the milk flow. The note deepens. Greyish white milk streams down the spout and raises froth in the bucket. After a while the cream, spun up through a series of perforated plates, begins to drop in a thin column into the bowl. It thickens as it cools. It is good-tasting cream but without the rich surprise of the clots in the mouth.

To make butter one allows the cream to cool for about twelve hours, then churns it in the one direction with a wooden beater. And wondrously, after a few minutes, the cream thickens and deepens in colour. One has stirred sunlight through it. After a few more turns the mass begins to sweat. It releases its buttermilk in a gush, and there is butter.

We buy cheese after much tasting, and we go back to those shopkeepers who know when their Brie is ripe. Press it and it should bulge, no more. It should not be firm like Gruyère, nor as runny as the inside of Stilton. It gives a crisp taste from a creamy texture, a gentle cheese. Some Gorgonzolas are brutal.

We buy yoghurt in Oxford Street, or Annandale, or Surry Hills, wherever Attiki yoghurt, the best in Australia, is sold. It is so good it never gets far from Marrickville where it is made. Whenever any members of the family come from Sydney they bring eskys of Attiki yoghurt. Sometimes we make our own yoghurt which is even better. Breakfast for me begins with yoghurt and homemade muesli of wheat germ, bran and several dried fruits varied each morning by a different fresh fruit.

And we buy coffee from Belaroma in Roseville, a joky shop with the best coffee. Sometimes one walks in through a dangle of silly message mugs. Green coffee has an odour, no taste. Roasting brings it to life. Perhaps for the absolute cup we should roast our own because once roasted it quickly loses its marvellous new attributes. But we get near perfection by mixing half a strong, dark roast called Caramel, and half a light brown, mild roast called Belaroma and

Taste

keeping the beans in sealed jars in either the refrigerator or the freezer according to how soon they will be used.

This method makes the best coffee. I heat water in a glass saucepan to 82°C, a temperature that does not drive off the volatile oils that bear the flavour. While the water is heating I grind the beans, a heaped teaspoon of powder to each mug. I measure it in graduated glass. Metal must not touch coffee. The filter paper is ready in the funnel over the warmed glass jug. I modify the funnels by making the small drain hole bigger, about six millimetres, and by boring two similar-sized holes each side of it. I throw the ground coffee into the heated water, swirl it round once or twice, and filter it quickly.

I like coffee mid-morning. After dinner it destroys the memory of the wines. And each of us has a favourite mug. Coffee out of someone else's mug tastes the wrong shape.

A woman who had been blind since birth and gained her sight in middle-age told me the most remarkable things she saw in the first week of seeing were the stacks of fruit and vegetables in greengrocers. Oranges rose in glowing pyramids built of balls of sunlight. She had thought of tomatoes as a chaste vegetable lacking passion. Boxes of them beckoned her with crimson promises. Lettuce folded secrets in deep green along with artichoke hearts and cabbages.

In New Guinea I walked into a native garden abandoned a month before by natives disorganised by the war. The papaw palms were loaded with fruit. They sagged to the ground with orange ovals thirty centimetres long. Many were overripe. They had split and leaked fermented juice. I picked a good fruit, sat on a stump, quartered it with my bayonet, and ate the lot. It was different, scented with New Guinea not Australia, but the best papaw I have eaten. And while I was eating, blue and black butterflies came to feast on the rotting fruit. They came over the top of the high jungle and drifted down into the clearing like falling petals – thousands of them. A dozen or more landed on each rotting fruit. The garden had broken into impossible blue bloom.

Modern vegetables are grown to pack well. The latest tomato looks good, it is firm and carries without bruising.

Celebration

Its skin is so thick it seems armour-plated and most of the flavour has gone. Spring onions are half the size of leeks and shaped like leeks. The bulb of subtle flavour curving up to a thin green stem is gone. All one has left is a coarse stalk that leaves a burning sensation in the mouth. Stringless beans are round and bloated. They can be washed and cooked whole without any tedious stringing. There is no inconvenience with the new bean, no taste.

For good fruit and vegetables one either has to grow one's own or seek out greengrocers like Parisi's in Sydney's West Ryde who know what fruit and vegetables ought to taste like. In season one can buy fresh dates there, from Israel early in our spring, then the big Californian dates later. Of necessity, they are frozen but they survive that savage process well, and as fresh dates they are a luscious new fruit, not a dried confection.

Among the sequence of green and brown pears in season, one finds the little green Corella pear splotched with pink and yellow. It grew from a seedling in the Barossa Valley in South Australia and adds a delicate new flavour to a marvellous fruit. Pears are elusive. None of their qualities can be defined. They need new words. Call the flesh crisp and an apple denies it. Call it luscious and an apricot denies it. Call it scented and a passionfruit denies it, sweet and a banana denies it, succulent and a pineapple denies it, juicy and an orange denies it. Call it the best fruit of all and a peach denies it. Calling it delicious lots it with so many fruit it means nothing.

The tart cooking apple known as Granny Smith also grew from a seedling. It came up by chance in old Granny Smith's backyard in Ryde, Sydney. She treasured it for the rest of her life and propagated it. As children we threaded these big green apples on wires and held them over red-hot coals as the open fire died at night. When they were brown in patches and the flesh bubbled through the skin, we slipped them on to plates, buttered them, and sprinkled them with sugar and cinnamon. Such apples might restore tired lovers but it was not apples that Solomon called on for comfort in his *Song*. The word was mistranslated. The old fruit was more like our apricot. And according to the Hindus, Eve

Taste

did not tempt Adam with an apple in their Sri Lankan paradise, but a banana.

A couple of years ago we ended a meal with a bottle of 1956 Chateau d'Yquem and white clingstone peaches. The peaches ripened on the tree and I had picked them early that morning with the dew on them. The wine is France's supreme Sauterne and 1956 was a good year. I bought it in 1960 when the price was ordinary. By the time we drank it twenty years later, it would have fetched hundreds of dollars at auction, a price that would make it such an outlandish indulgence it would introduce overtones to the palate. We tasted nothing but peaches and Sauternes. The peaches were perfect. The wine had gone golden in colour and had thickened slightly. It was so sweet it seemed to have concentrated sweetness towards some infinite point. But it was not the heavy sweetness of honey. It was so light it left the palate early. What we had as after-taste were young Australian peaches and exquisitely matured French grapes.

Hunter Valley semillon, especially Lindeman's, changes from light green to straw colour at ten years – the colour of the old bottle envelopes stitched up out of oaten stubble. It develops a slight wet-straw flavour then, too, that fits the clean, delicate fruit of the wine. The wine fits scallops or crabs at the beginning of a meal. It keeps on improving up to about the fifteenth year and no imported wine can take its place.

South Australian Rhine Riesling develops more quickly. At six or seven years the best of the Orlando vintages are beautifully complex wines that can accompany the richest pork and chicken dishes. The 1979 Petaluma Rhine Riesling might finish even better. It was made in the Clare Valley by Brian Croser, a young winemaker who uses old methods. He made no chemical tests for sugar-acid balance, he tasted his grapes. When all the other growers picked in February as sugar levels rose, he continued tasting. The sugar level was right but the taste was not. He picked at the end of March. Then, scorning the available yeasts to ferment his must, he cultured his own from the fungi on the grapes. Perhaps grapes for white wine in Australia are usually picked too soon.

Celebration

Early in 1972 Grant Burge and Ian Wilson, the new young winemakers from Southern Vales Co-operative Winery at McLaren Vale in South Australia, were confronted by an angry rival winemaker. 'You young bastards! You've not only pinched my cabernet, you've buggered it up. You picked before it was ripe.' Red grapes then were in short supply. They suspected a contract grower had overestimated his crop and they made sure they picked first to secure their fourteen tonnes. The wine they made was the 1972 Tatachilla Cabernet Sauvignon, a rarely good wine. Perhaps grapes for red wine are often picked too late, and the wines, instead of developing with acid, remain bitter with tannin accentuated by too much oak.

The best of the Hunter Valley Shiraz keeps and develops. Wines that Dan Tyrrell and Maurice O'Shea made in the 1940s and 1950s would still be keeping and developing in a few good cellars. Lindeman's reds of the early 1960s are superbly delicate wines with just that touch of earthiness to prove the vine grew in soil. A Latour can follow with its marvellously controlled robustness, or a Châteauneuf-du-Pape, earthier, deeper red and almost furry (it is good to bring together tastes from the two hemispheres), or else a Balgownie Cabernet from Bendigo in Victoria, another young vineyard producing some of Australia's best, or a Penfold's Grange Hermitage, one of the world's great wines. But the last vintage of that wine has been bottled. The bulldozers have moved in and Adelaide is spreading over the vineyard as finally as phylloxera.

Sometimes the earthiness of Hunter Valley reds becomes slight mustiness: the sweaty saddle nose. On the first couple of sips it tastes good. Then one realises the flavour builds up and lingers till it is the final flavour. And the final flavour of wine should be fruit.

I open wine with a double-acting wooden screw John Thompson, the poet, gave me about 1949. He had bought it in Paris. How many thousand bottles has it opened? And there was excitement in opening every one. I never open a bottle of wine inattentively. Even the modest wines we drink every day are carefully chosen. When the cork is drawn, after the quick sniff at the top of the bottle to test for soundness, they are worth a longer, enjoyable sniff, and

Taste

then an hour in a wide-mouthed decanter to lift them. Some waiters present the cork to smell. I ask for the bottle. I enjoy smelling wine, I do not enjoy smelling cork. The smell of wine makes one want to drink it. The smell of cork does not make one want to eat it.

When I open a good bottle of wine, I am conscious of the time treasured in it: ten, fifteen, twenty years for the vines to reach their best, a year or two in the making and the cask, then five, fifteen, twenty years and more in the bottle. What I release is the quality of one year many years before, of a moonlit night's picking, of the busy crushing, of the quick fermentation of the must, the stirrings and the knocking down of the hat that rises to the surface, of the long, slow fermentation in oaken casks where the flavours develop, the bottling, the ullaging to stop oxidisation, then the gentle completion in the bottle where the flavours merge and entangle. Draw the cork and old memories rise from the bottle.

The memories need airing and settling down in a wide-mouthed jar. I opened two bottles of 1971 Grange four hours before we were to drink it. I decanted one bottle, the other stood open. Both wines were good. Only the decanted wine was memorable. We have two favourite decanting jars. Neither of them can be bought in Australia. The decanters sold here are made to the concept of the whisky decanter, a narrow-necked flask with a stopper in it to keep the air from the whisky. Leaving out the stopper does not air wine.

One of our decanters is heavy crystal. The base is solid and wide and the top about nine centimetres across. It shows off the wine as a set ruby. The other is a cylinder of the finest crystal about nine centimetres in diameter and slightly waisted at the top for a hand grip. It displays a crimson column of wine that seems to stand up by itself. It is so fragile one fears for it and fears for the wine, but a lovely thing.

Different wines need different airing times. Napa Valley Cabernet on opening is dead – no nose, no taste. Give it twelve hours in the decanter and it tells gusty Californian stories. It is rare for white wines to respond to decanting. Some Californian Chardonnays need twenty-four hours. Decant an aged Châteauneuf-du-Pape for four hours and all that is left is a bit of old velvet. Give it twenty minutes and it brings the spirit of

Celebration

Avignon to your table. A Margaux or a Pauillac need more time, one to three hours according to the age of the wine. Any wine fifty years old is too delicate for airing. Australian wines need one to four hours – Grange and the old Hunter Rivers the longest.

In getting out the wines for a dinner party one looks at labels, remembers, savours the wine through the bottles. This one for that dish, that for this. What order do we drink them in? I give a quick sniff at each decanter to check my judgement. That quick sniff is reliable. Go back and compare with long sniffs. One gets lost. Try tasting. Unless one is prepared to taste like a wine taster, and spit the wine out and cleanse the palate before tasting the next, tasting is hopeless. And I am not going to spit out a mouthful of wine I have treasured for years. But after the decision is made, once the decanters are arranged in order, then one can appreciate the wine all afternoon. Walk past, bend over one decanter, take a long breath. Walk back, bend over another. Our guests are usually house guests so they do not miss out either. How much of the wine do we take with our noses?

Tall-stemmed wineglasses look good but shape, provided it is spacious and does not dissipate the nose, is not important. What matters is the quality of the crystal. The glass should display the wine, not itself. So the walls must be thin and plain. Hollow-stemmed champagne glasses are kitsch. My big nose snags on the popular narrow tulips. Champagne is best out of crystal water glasses.

I love to go to restaurants. We do not go often. When we do go, the night is memorable. But the best food is one's own cooking. Stuff the snapper one has caught with chopped oysters, bake it, make a sauce of white wine and the pan juices, garnish with green beans, and how could fish taste better? Or cut a lid in the top of a perfect pumpkin leaving the broken-off stem as a handle. Scoop out the seeds, stuff with breadcrumbs, butter, chopped onions, nutmeg (very little), sage, a bay leaf, salt, pepper, grated Gruyère cheese and two or three cups of thick cream. Seal with the lid and bake for about an hour and a half till the outside softens and the inside is bubbly. Bring it to the table. Outside is plebeian pumpkin. Inside is wonder.

The best of Australia's restaurants are good. But the food is seldom so good it stills conversation. One eats with delight but

Taste

not wonder. Six to eight is a good number at table – one bottle of wine fills the glasses. Fewer limits the range of wines. A greater number disorders conversation. It gets spilt all round the table.

What one remembers mostly at a restaurant is the atmosphere. For a couple of years after Patric Juillet opened Le Café Nouveau in Paddington as a small restaurant one remembers enthusiasm – for the food, for the diners, for the wines which were excellent. We drank superb French white there we did not know. And we ate lamb younger than we had ever eaten it and found the milky flavour interesting. And we marvelled at the yabbies. No strip of flesh had been lifted off the tail so the thick black gut could be removed. How did he take it out? Patric did not take it out. He bought his yabbies alive and fed them oatmeal for four days to cleanse the gut.

We remember the more formal enjoyment at Fanny's in Melbourne and the modelled puddings one studies before eating; and Stephanie's vigorous Indian-Malay hostess who comes out and does a spiel about the food that makes everyone even hungrier. Stephanie Alexander says her cooking is to the left of *haute cuisine* with a touch of housewife. It is good. And the great old house in Hawthorn that contains the restaurant is very beautiful.

One remembers the good jazz and good soups at Soup Plus in George Street, Sydney, a simple place; and even simpler, before it became self-conscious, No Names in Darlinghurst: no telephone, no name, no number, just a door in a wall, a cement floor, and a narrow staircase; and upstairs, cheap tables and chairs in a big room noisy with a marvellous assortment of people. Walk past six tables and hear six languages. There are families with children down to babies in baskets, shift workers in blue overalls, businessmen with briefcases, couples in evening dress, children in private school uniforms, university students – people with most of the colours and shapes of faces in existence. They bring in their own bottles of wine, flagons, plastic casks, even, great heavens! a little wooden cask of home made wine. Tall, rough, northern Italian waiters move among them serving good spaghetti and salad, or bearing armfuls of crusty bread to fill the baskets on the tables.

We went to a Turkish restaurant, Uskudar, in Melbourne's Brunswick. I booked for Thursday. The voice on the telephone

Celebration

said 'Ah! Come Friday. There is a belly-dancer on Friday. Half past nine.' We booked for 7.30 on Friday thinking the belly-dancer would conclude the meal. The proprietor was his own cook and much of the time his own waiter. He came to the table. 'You don't know anything about Turkish cooking' he said, 'you don't need a menu. I'll bring you food.' We waited for half an hour, drinking the wine we had brought. He carried in three dishes each, very small servings. 'Hungry?' he asked. 'This is planned to make you hungrier.' We did not know what we were eating. He explained but we could not understand all he said. It was good. Small balls of green leaves had rice flavoured with glycerine in the centre. In another twenty minutes a fish dish came, strangely and interestingly spiced. There was another long wait, then a more substantial serving of sliced lamb with okra in a tomato sauce.

Nothing happened for so long after that we thought the meal had ended. Then a waitress came in with a couple of light, different servings and soon after she came with more. Joan talked to her. We found she was the proprietor's wife. She had attended a university in Turkey for a couple of years but she was not a good student. And her ideas were too modern for Turkish society. 'Turkish men' she said, 'they are too dominant. They like to shut us up as breeders. My husband is different. We have a good life here.' The restaurant was full but she was unhurried. It was past time for the belly-dancer. We asked if she was coming. 'Ah, yes! Here later. Little bit late tonight.' She or her husband brought in other small servings at irregular intervals, perhaps one spiced meat ball on a plate or rice with some vegetable threaded through it. Each fresh dish was unexpected. Each new flavour seemed to carry on from the last. Each was delivered with a broad smile.

At a quarter to eleven music started. The belly-dancer spun in. It was a chaste belly dance – the accent did not drop from her belly to her cunt – but she was very good. She leapt on to tables dancing, leapt off. She inched down the floor arched backwards with her hands on the floor behind her head. All that seemed to be moving was her belly. We thought we recognised the wife and waitress and watched her closely. She spun past us, tapped me on the shoulder, said 'Yes, yes! It's me' and danced on. Astonishingly, after the dance, a couple of rich meat dishes arrived. We felt sure the meal had ended. We sat and talked for twenty minutes. I rose to pay. The till was in the hall away from the dining room. The proprietor stood there. Other couples had just gone out. 'Ah, but you cannot go yet' he said, 'your coffee, you have not had your coffee. Or your little sweet cakes.' We talked some more and waited. The strong, fragrant, furry Turkish coffee did come, and very sweet light cakes.

At midnight when we both rose to go, there were not many diners left. There was no one waiting for our money in the hall, nor in the kitchen. We heard voices and laughter from another room. I walked through the kitchen, parted curtains. The proprietor, his wife and several friends were drinking coffee at a table. 'That was a marvellous meal' I said. 'Would you like some money?' 'Too soon again!' said the proprietor. 'In another ten minutes it would have been on the house.'

I remember one flavour only from that meal: the few drops of glycerine in the rice. It fitted the oils of the salads and grains, the tang of the meats. We ate exceedingly well. But even better, while we ate a careless gaiety slowly absorbed us. We drove home laughing.

Hearing

We wake to bird calls. In army training camps the first notes of reveille jerked us out of sleep at 6 a.m. Tent flaps lifted, cranky soldiers cursed the bugler. 'Blow your guts out, you bastard!' 'Jam the fuckin' thing down his throat!' 'Stick it up his arse and play retreat!' During the war in Papua New Guinea, when I woke a signaller to take the next night watch, I stood off and nudged him with a long stick. The Japanese were very close. We manned our radio in a hidden dugout and all of us were on edge. Bend over a man and wake him suddenly and he would come up ready to kill. In cities there is little difference in night noise and day noise. Most of it is mechanical and jarring. Daylight is veiled by buildings, by shadows, by unnatural cloud. So I must waken to a jangling alarm. In the country the timber walls, the galvanised iron roof do not insulate us from outdoors. Sounds come in unimpeded through open doors on wide gauzed verandahs, through open gauzed windows. I waken gladly to bird calls.

All through the night in brief wakings one hears birds. When nesting the male Willie Wagtail maintains his territory day and night. 'Sweet pretty little creature' he calls. The words sound too definite and metallic, like the electronic voice of a robot. From a tree a couple of hundred metres away another male proclaims his territory. 'What a pretty creature! Pretty little creature.' Another busy black and white bird, the Restless Flycatcher, stops grating out his daytime scissors-grinder notes and instead calls musically 'Jury. Jury. Jury.' Sometimes one wakes to strange cackling laughter. A Spotted Nightjar that did not catch enough insects at dusk is on the wing again, hawking. When a Horsefield Bronze Cuckoo is about it whistles its drawn-out downward note unceasingly. Most cuckoos call musically but none know when to stop. The Pallid Cuckoo arrives in the spring with a lovely rising five-note song. Even though

Hearing

he never calls by night, after the first few days we curse him as the Brainfever Bird. Occasionally a Boobook Owl perches on a corner of the guttering. 'Morepork. Morepork' he calls. From forest and farm timber belts his rivals answer him like ricocheting echoes, 'Morepork, morepork'.

Each season has its own alarm. In winter the cling-clang of Pied Currawongs wakes us fittingly after the sun is well up and the frost has begun to melt. Then a chorus of Pied Butcher-birds guarantees a good morning. Six or seven birds ring the house in widely-spaced trees. One sings a few notes, another takes it up, all join in to the end of the air. They sing six different tunes, one of them eight bars long.

In autumn when the sunflowers are ripe, two thousand galahs awaken us. They come in rolling pink and grey clouds as noisy as thunder. They turn screaming catherine wheels on the electric light wires, they chew off the lead to the television aerial, they strip leaves off the eucalypts in the windbreak and toss them down, they slither along the iron roof of the house, scraping and screeching. Then they fly into the paddock and eat sunflowers.

In spring so many birds wake us we have to concentrate to recognise them all. The White-winged Triller makes long rolls of two notes. The Rufous Whistler makes a few musical calls, then cracks like a whip, a good alarm. The little Striated Pardalote beats out its two notes astonishingly loudly. One nests in the open-ended fifty millimetre piping that supports the trusses of one of the sheds. When the female flies in calling to her young ones, the pipe channels her cries and they issue from the end like blasts from a horn. Three species of doves and two of pigeons murmur and bubble. They soothe the morning. The Grey Shrike-thrush excites it with marvellous harmonies. And Double-bar Finches keep in touch by sighing to one another plaintively as they suck their first morning drink where an old rainwater tank leaks onto a cement path.

In summer we are woken early. At the first suggestion of daylight, before one can be certain the east is lightening, the Rufous Songlark throbs a succession of notes. Then for half an hour before anything else stirs, he chirrs and whistles and sings as though he is several birds. The parrots wake up, and the raucous Noisy Friar-bird chortling 'Scratch

Celebration

your cock', and several other species of honeyeaters. And the White-tailed Warbler, a little bird with a big voice, sings its sweet, unfinished cadence. The day has begun, it seems to say, but it doesn't know where it's going.

As I sit writing, a male Superb Blue Wren makes a morning inspection of the gauze on the open window thirty centimetres from my shoulder. I face away from windows, away from distraction. But I turn round to watch that blue scrap clinging there and cleaning up little insects trapped the night before. By night the gauze is patrolled by geckos. I hear those plump little lizards, too: a rustle as padded feet make a quick charge, then the snap of jaws as a moth disappears.

Sometimes I hear vigorous scratching beneath the rosemary bush immediately outside the long window. Our family of nine Brown Quail, both parents and seven grown young ones, are prospecting for dropped seeds. They work in a group, then run off in line, whistling softly to each other to keep contact.

The house lets in the noise of wind, too. We hear the trees shake. We hear the discarded leaves of the Kurrajongs and Silky Oaks land on the roof. We hear the windmill turning with a few little squeaks two hundred metres away, and the pump rod change direction with a soft thud ten to twenty times a minute. Best of all we hear the rain on the roof, first the scattered drops like instruments tuning, then the oratorio as grand as one by Handel. But at harvest time when there are uncovered and vulnerable bins of grain in the paddock, an unexpected scatter of raindrops on the roof brings us out of bed with a leap and we run for the Land-Rover with its load of tarpaulins to haul over the bins.

The first raindrops in Australia's central deserts plop out of sight in the loose sand. They might be little stones falling. Dust kicks up from them. When the surface of the ground is wet, the rain drums on it. Then a smell comes up – a warm, clean, keen smell of gibberellin, acids and oils. It smells exciting, like things growing. And things do grow. Bare sand springs lush green in five days.

In the early 1960s I heard a Hungarian gypsy orchestra conducted by Alexandre Pecsi play in Sydney. They played brilliantly. It was a night that grew gladness. Towards the

Hearing

end of the programme they played that old showpiece, 'The Skylark'. It was a marvel. We saw skylarks rising from the stage. The musicians excelled themselves, and both musicians and audience were excited. The applause lasted many minutes. Pecsi announced they were concluding with the csárdás, Hungarian tavern dances that begin slowly and end wildly. Gypsy orchestras use the music as linking pieces between more formal works or as a gay ending. They played the last part of the csárdás only, a merry movement, and they played it quickly. There was applause. They played it again and played it quicker. There was prolonged applause. They played it quicker and left the stage. The audience clapped so long they came back and played it quicker. The notes were perfect. It did not seem possible to play so quickly. The hands bowing the violins moved in a blur. They left the stage. The audience clapped. A fifth time, a sixth time they came back and each time they played quicker. The audience stood and cheered. They called 'More! More!' They clapped and clapped and clapped. And with the whole audience standing in excitement the orchestra came back a seventh time and played it quicker. When they were finished the musicians put down their instruments and hugged one another. Pecsi bowed to his violinists and embraced them all together. All of them clapped and jigged and shouted and ran about the stage. I feared for the instruments apparently lying there forgotten but none was trodden on. In the end the musicians lined up across the stage, hands on each other's shoulders, and the audience cheered them.

Beethoven excites more deeply. He leaves one marvelling silently. One has heard something beyond full understanding. He proposes worlds of sounds out of reach. In high school I wondered at the worlds within reach: the different keys of Indian music, the changing times and abruptly cut-off rhythm of Hebridean folk-songs, the unconventional gaiety of Percy Grainger's piano pieces. He lifted happy folk-dances into regions of deep joy. Louis Armstrong picked up his trumpet and pulled centuries together. Shadrach, Meshach, Abednego – the Old Testament characters lived in modern times. We knew Ezekiel, saw wheels turning in the air.

Celebration

I have never had enough music. I play with words, not musical notes. In music I could only admire what someone else had done. I had to build for myself.

Grass Whistle-Ducks follow flood rains in big, musical flocks. One hears them fly over like an orchestra of wind instruments. Their wings whistle, they call in whistles. The wings beat an unchanging drone that harmonises with a shrill, pulsing treble as duck whistles to duck. Now and again two or three birds at a time whistle a long, loud, piercing note that silences the twittering momentarily.

Chinese pigeon-keepers in the extravagant feudal days fitted their birds with little silver and bamboo whistles tuned to different notes, and released them to fly harmonies. Modern Chinese men tell of kite-flying in their youths and the little one-or-two-stringed bamboo harps they fitted to them so that they hummed as they flew.

Early one winter morning I walked out onto the frosty lawn. The world was frozen still. I heard a leaf drop and at once I had this poem. I went inside and wrote it down, fearful it would go as quickly as it came. I called it 'Deciduous'.

> Frost still, and the leaves brittle.
> You'd not expect to hear them rattle
> From broken stem, to twig, to branch
> And down to earth with a tiny crunch
>
> Of crystals on the frozen lawn
> Drab by a five o'clock sinking moon.
> You know the wind can make them sound
> By a multiple scraping on the ground,
>
> But one leaf is such a little thing
> You'd not expect to hear it falling.
> I heard the break, the drop, the landing
> Clear as a word, and I wasn't listening.

We finished one bout of lovemaking with my head resting against her groin. She was very wet and profoundly excited. Amazingly, I heard her orgasm. The walls of her vagina smacked together. Even after the strong rolling contractions were over, the last well-spaced single spasms were audible.

Hearing

We had then been married twenty years. Joan never loses the capacity to amaze me.

The Aborigines of the Barramundi fish group in Arnhem Land sing of the penis talking: it is scented with the juices of the girl and it slides forward talking. Their penises might make unusual squelching noises. The last few centimetres are split open on the underside as deeply as the urethra. When the penis erects the glans flares out and ridges. It is the shape of a fish, they sing. The Barramundi swims up the creek.

Many tribes in northern and central Australia practised the strange initiation rite of sub-incision. Not many tribes are now intact enough to practise anything. Different tribes split the underside of the penis different ways. Some opened it from root to tip and it erected into a half cylinder. Others merely opened up two or three centimetres in the middle and it bulged there like a faulty bicycle tube. Whites termed them whistle cocks. The operation had the odd effect of causing the penis to emit a high-pitched whistle during urination. The sound varied with the length of the split. The men of each tribe pissed a different note.

Sub-incision has no contraceptive effect but it does cause much of the semen to dribble around the vulva, especially as most of the women prefer lovemaking from behind. 'Fuck me till your semen drips from my clitoris!' The girls roll their shoulders, jiggle their breasts, flaunt their buttocks to attract the men. 'Fuck me till you mat my pubic hair!' They are imaginative as well as matter-of-fact. When a Barramundi girl rides on top she says she is rowing her canoe. She speaks of her vulva eating the penis, or of roasting and eating the snake. An Aranda tribesman told his mate her vulva was a flower full of nectar. Most of the flowers are now dead. When Aranda men went out to fight, the nursing women fitted them with symbolic armour. They stood in line, lifted their breasts, and sprayed the men with milk as they ran past.

I ran the gauntlet of the street girls at Sydney's Kings Cross. That fleshly carnival was once a good place to relax in after a day's research at the library. Now it it unsafe to walk there alone late at night. One has to be too careful where one looks. Eye contact is a challenge to the new

Celebration

young muggers. The grubby girls were always there, wilting on street corners, beckoning from doorways, leaning back in enervated poses against brick walls. Lone males were fair game. 'Hey mate! Do yer wanna girl?' Their voices carried little invitation, no expectation. I could not conceive of any degree of lust that would cause me to accept. Plenty of men did. A group of drunken sailors picked their girls like fruit off a shelf, bore them in a tight knot to a half-open doorway, unravelled themselves in pairs and threaded their way inside. A very short man chose a very tall girl. She set off briskly down the street with him hurrying behind her, a lily swaying away from a bee.

One girl I passed worked from the gutter side of the footpath. She looked younger and more hopeful than the other girls. 'Hey Fatty!' she called, 'Would you like twenty minutes exercise?' She startled me. It was the first time I realised I had put on weight. 'No thank you' I said, 'what I must need is less to eat.' I left her laughing, and surely there would not be too much to laugh at in her job.

Laughter is missing in masturbation. It is an imperative exercise. But I am sceptical about it as an art with props of pillows, mirrors, oils, vibrators, music, films. There is no one to react with, to share marvels or mishaps. Surely no man, no woman can ever have stopped in the middle of their lone urgent fiddling to roll about a bed laughing. Lovemaking can be very funny.

We were north-west of Bourke on a little-used track, a long way into the flat interior of Australia. Our recently-weaned daughter and her brother had been left with my parents while we had a holiday looking round back roads. It was winter and we stopped for a picnic lunch where the overhead sun warmed a clearing in the hopbush scrub. And after we packed the food away, we undressed and coupled doggy style on the rug. It was marvellous. Warmth radiated within us from our moving genitals. Warmth rose from the ground to meet us. The sun caressed my buttocks like warmed hands. Balls hung at summer length and swung rhythmically. Her pubic hair received them, cushioned them, teased them. We seemed to be focussing warmth towards some exquisite point.

Her cunt began to fart. There were high-pitched squeaks

and low-pitched groans. Perhaps her vagina was still a little slack after giving birth and she sucked in more air than is usual in that position. She was embarrassed. 'Oh dear! That's awful!' The note varied with the depth of stroke. 'I wonder if we could play the Anvil Chorus?' A slow deep stroke produced a long vibrating blast. We began to laugh. We shouted and wobbled with laughter, clutching at each other to keep connected. At last she said 'Stop laughing now. You're shrivelling up and I want to go off.' So she turned on her back and we concentrated as seriously as we could.

An hour later when we had dressed and were folding up the rug, we heard a car coming. Incongruously an old open car drove by loaded with tennis players dressed all in white, shouting, laughing, waving their rackets over the doors. What were they doing in such high spirits? Where were they going? Early that morning many kilometres back we had passed a group of village tennis courts where a tournament was about to begin but they were much too late to compete there. And the vehicle was thirty years old. The party seemed simply to have driven out of the irresponsible 1920s and lost its way on an Australian bush track in 1957.

When sleeper cars were attached to country trains they were a good way to travel. No time was lost in travelling. One boarded the train at bed-time and slept till one arrived at the destination. Once during one of those mysterious night halts of trains I woke as the engine jerked to a stop and let off steam. I was in a top bunk and a woman's voice came clearly from the top bunk in the next compartment through a crack in the corner of the dividing wall. 'Bert. Hey Bert! Come up and give us a cuddle.'

Bert in the bottom bunk replied sleepily 'Aw!'

'I don't want yer to do nothin', Bert. I just want a cuddle.'

'There's no room. I'd bloody fall out.'

'Me bum's cold, Bert.'

Then the train started and the reply of her reluctant lover was lost in the scrape of steel on steel.

Through five years of school in Sydney, through a couple of frustrating years of mainland army, I got on trains, off trains, changed trains at all hours of the day and night. At 4.15 one morning at a country junction I stretched out on a

Celebration

seat to wait for a connecting train. The stationmaster and his assistant in the nearby office were catching up on some returns.

''Ere, get these, will yer Bill? Are yer there Bill? 'Ere, Bill, get these will yer.'

'Yair. All right.'

The stationmaster began to read: 'Truck number 4372C ex Darling 'Arbour...' He read a full sheet of figures and destinations and loadings in a monotonous sing-song. ''Ave yer got that?'

'Got what?'

'Gawd! Didn't yer get it?'

'Nah.'

'You was supposed to write 'em down.'

'Aw.'

'Git one of them forms there – no, one of them others. Yair, that's the one. Orright now. Are yer ready? Well 'ere, get this. Truck number 4372C ex Darling 'Arbour...'

The modern electric trams of Melbourne and Adelaide are an efficient and uninteresting mode of public transport. Somewhere they lost their character, and attempts at spectacular painting make them self-conscious rather than distinctive. The old trams that Sydney so foolishly discarded were unmodern, uncomfortable, unfailing – they ran to time – and, even in dilapidation, they were eccentrically lively. They rocked along to the grinding of steel and the clang of the little unmusical bell the conductor pulled once to signal the driver to stop if he was moving, or to move if he was stopped. Now and again there were bursts of static from jumping sparks as the overhead pulley that picked up the current rode across intersecting wires.

The oldest trams were the toast-rack type, compartmented pairs of seats facing one another. The conductor worked from the running-board. 'Fezz pliz! Fezz pliz!' he called. The cry carried. No projection of 'fares please' could have been heard as clearly. So many English words lose themselves in short distances.

Paper-boys were masters of cries. 'Paper! Paper! The *Sun* or *Mirror*!' An old-time Shakespearian actor could not have made those words carry. 'Pay-yer! Pay-yer!' called the boys, 'Sunnamirra! Sunnamirra!' The words carried the length of streets. Those barefoot boys leapt out of a more agile world than I ever belonged to. They danced between moving cars, skipped onto the moving trams, sold papers, jumped off again among the traffic, dodging cars as skilfully as bullfighters.

We boarded steam trains to the chanting of destinations: 'Strathfield, 'Ornsby, and all points north ter Moree. Strathfield, 'Ornsby...' The voice died away down the length of the train. And hours later in early morning darkness another guard with a hand-held lantern called at Narrabri Junction: 'Passergers for the western branch must change 'ere. All those passergers for Walgett, Pokataroo.' If a curious and unknowing passenger had got off and boarded for Pokataroo he would have found nothing but an unattended wooden platform little longer than the name swimming in the shimmering mirages of black-soil plains.

I heard the last cries of the clothes-prop seller in Marrickville. Shortage of handy timber, then the new Hills Hoists put him out of business long before I had finished school. But when every backyard had a forked wooden pole to prop up a slack wire line, the clothes-prop sellers with laden horse-drawn drays found plenty of customers. 'Claars perrops! Claars perrops!' they called.

The rabbit-ohs with their clean, clear calls lasted longer than the clothes-prop sellers. The furred but gutted rabbits hung head-down in pairs from racks on horse-drawn drays. The call died for fifty years. Now one hears it again on Saturday mornings at Melbourne's Victoria Market. 'Rabbit-oh! Rabbit-oh! 'Ole or minced!' The rabbits still hang in pairs from racks as they have been hung for one hundred and twenty years. Small racks of hares hang beside them. Tuesdays, Thursdays and Fridays the stall-holders sell sedately. They behave like conventional shopkeepers. Sunday is a rest day for the sellers of food. So on Saturday mornings they market energetically and raucously. 'Ever tried a rabbit rissole, ma'am? Sunday night yer don't want a blow-out. Try yer old man with a rabbit rissole. Rabbit-oh! Rabbit-oh!'

Near by the butchers parade outside their stalls holding up unsold cuts of meat. 'Here's a nice slab of steak, lady.

Celebration

'Five dollars the lot. There's two and a half kilos of steak 'ere, lady. You won't do better than that. It's all topside. 'Ere, 'ave a look. Get yer weekend meat 'ere cheap. It's all gotta go. We're clearin' out the stall. Well, four dollars fifty then, lady. 'Ere y'are! It's a good buy. I'll cut it up for yer if you like.'

We walked past a tray of green beans. They looked good, so Joan reached out, picked one up and tested it between her fingers. It broke reluctantly so she dropped it back uninterestedly. The stallholder saw her and pulled the tray protectively closer. 'That's the last bean what gets broke today, missus.'

Cattle sales begin with the cry 'Sale-oh! Sale-oh!' The auctioneer and his retinue mount the catwalk that runs above the pens. There is a bookkeeper with clipboard and biro, two or three assistants with notebooks to count out and give delivery, a yardman with a long cane. As the buyers collect in the lane in front of the pens one of the assistants reads the Conditions of Sale: all stock shall be at the risk and expense of the purchaser upon the fall of the hammer; the vendor reserves the right of making one bid for each lot. It is a long list of legalities and technicalities that must be read aloud to legalise the sale. Nobody listens to the unfortunate reader. Everybody has heard it too often though no one knows much of what is in it. Aware of the disinterest the reader gabbles through it. Then the auctioneer takes over. He is an actor, a showman, an everlasting optimist. If the country is flooded, well, next week will be fine and the grass will grow amazingly. If there is drought he finds somewhere a forecast of good rains. He conducts his buyers, lifts bids like musical notes.

'Every beast advertised is yarded here today, gentlemen. And you'll agree you seldom see cattle of this quality yarded. There are trucks available to move them and we'll give delivery during the course of the sale. Now this first pen, gentlemen, is a draft of four-year-old cows from Collymungle station.' The yardman jumps down among them and smacks the nearest rump with the leather clapper on his cane. He stirs the cows about so the buyers can see them all. Cattle do not like being crowded together. Some try to butt others out of the way, some drop their heads in bewilderment under adjacent bellies, some snort and shake their heads at the human faces looking at them through the rails. Urine splashes, manure squirts from uneasy bowels. There is the warm, acidic, mouldering grass smell of cattle.

'These cows are pregnancy-tested in calf to four thousand dollar bulls. You don't often get Herefords of this quality offered, gentlemen. It is only the season that makes them available. There are thirty in the pen, the next two pens are the same cattle, a genuine run-off. I'm offering this one pen with the option of two or three. They'll make over three hundred dollars, gentlemen. Have you got three hundred dollars to start? They're worth every cent.'

Someone calls 'Two hundred'. The auctioneer knows his values. 'No way, sir. They're worth more than that to the butcher. Two-eighty! Thank you sir.' Someone else has called a bid. 'Two-eighty I'm bid, five! Two-ninety, two-ninety. Is that a bid? Five! Two-ninety-five. Three hundred! Three hundred I've got. It's in the corner. Against you, sir. They're worth another bid. Five. Ten.' He points towards the quick bids. 'Three-ten I've got. Are you done?' The auctioneer and his assistants move their heads like birds watching for insects. Buyers make a game of almost imperceptible bids. But a good auctioneer can pick up the wink of one left eye among three hundred eyes, a one-centimetre raise of a little finger, a flick of a thumb.

'Fifteen! It's against you now, sir. Three-fifteen dollars. Are you done? Done?' He knows they have reached their value so he does not dwell. His outstretched hands widen. 'Done!' he calls for the third time and his hands clap together. And once they have closed on that third call no bid may prise them open.

Immediately he moves towards the next pen calling out the name of the buyer as he goes and praising the next pen. He remembers faces, remembers names. 'This is another draft of the Collymungle cows, same age, same breeding, just a little lighter in condition. All they want's a feed. I want two-eighty to start.' He conducts emotion and reason, hope, greed, knowledge, competitiveness, dignity, egotism, need, opportunism, acumen. He orchestrates them all to a final, sweet-sounding bid.

In the 1970s an auctioneer from Quirindi went to Sydney

Celebration

to sell a house for a local client who did not trust unknown city auctioneers. He expected the house to make a hundred thousand dollars. The auctioneer could not coax an opening bid from the strange faces before him so, with a conjuror's knowledge that silence is death to the trick, he began confidently at eighty thousand dollars and pulled in quick imaginary bids to a hundred thousand. Then he slowed down, praised the house between calls. 'It's dirt cheap at a hundred and ten thousand, a gift. It's brick, not brick veneer. Do I hear a hundred and fifteen?'

At one hundred and twenty thousand dollars he expected to call a fictitious name and leave the house unsold. But he acted out the auction to the last. 'A hundred and twenty thousand I've got. It's against you, sir.' He waved towards one of his imaginary bidders. 'A hundred and twenty thousand. All done? Done? A hundred and...' Someone in the audience half raised a hand. 'A hundred and twenty-five thousand. New blood!' said the auctioneer, disguising his relief at first blood. 'One twenty-five, one twenty-five.' Then someone else at the back called out 'Thirty' and the house was sold.

The buyer sauntered over to the auctioneer's table. He wore a pair of torn khaki shorts and thongs, nothing else. 'I'm a builder,' he explained. 'Just bought it on spec. Didn't think yer'd know me or me cheque book so I brought the deposit along in cash.' From his bulging back pocket he pulled a roll of fifty-dollar notes and counted out thirteen thousand dollars.

In 1928 – I was five years old – I went with my parents to hear a radio broadcast. Friends had bought what for years we called a wireless set. The event was a disappointing marvel. The origin of the music was mystery enough but the music itself was scratchy and interrupted by static. I still have no patience with imperfect machinery.

With that strange, inbuilt, immediate understanding of new machinery that allows twelve-year-old schoolboys in the 1980s to build computers, people all over the world began making their own wireless sets, simple crystal sets at first with reception limited to the wave-length of the crystal, then big tunable valve sets with up to eight glowing oval

Hearing

blue or clear globes plugged into multi-holed sockets. Soon there was a medley of radio waves for the wondrous new machines to collect and distinguish.

One of my uncles built our first wireless, a cumbersome thing fitted into an ornate walnut veneer cabinet about a metre high and seventy centimetres wide. It was powered by a six-volt wet-plate battery that had to be charged each week, so we used two batteries in rotation. We could pick up the Australian Broadcasting Commission's new station in Sydney; we could pick up Mark Oliver's VK 2MO Gunnedah.

Marcus Oliver was a garage proprietor and a remarkable self-taught engineer. He sold radios as a profitable sideline to the garage, then built his own transmitter in a corner of the dining-room of his home. The station opened in 1930. Mark took the morning shift, his wife the afternoon. His principal act of the day was the reading of the news at 7.30 each morning. He had a high, rough, sing-song voice and false faith in himself as a humorist. The news readings were bizarre.

'A war's broken out overseas at some little place I can't pronounce so we won't worry too much about that one. It's a long way from us, any'ow. A car ran off the 'Ume 'Ighway near Goulburn about 8 p.m. last night and ten people were injured. It says 'ere "ten of its passengers". There might've been more in it. What'd all those people be doing in one car? It must've looked like a sardine tin on wheels...

'Now we come to the advertisements.' He accented the third syllable. ' "Woman to cook and clean. No washing or ironing." They must be a dirty lot in that 'ousehold. Any'ow if you want the job, ring...'

The range of the station was astonishing. People as far away as Darwin tuned into that early morning news. As children we liked to sit up till the station went off the air at 10 p.m. Sometimes Mrs Oliver would say good night and forget to turn the transmitter off. We would hear the hiss from the live carrier-wave, the rustle of papers as she tidied up. Then shortly a door would open and Mark would shout 'Hey missus! Have you turned the bloody thing off yet?'

The pronouncement of World War II came over that set

Celebration

my uncle made. Two years later I was signalling by radio in the Australian army, at first in a Light Horse regiment. We wore our wide-brimmed felt hats with the brim clipped up on the left-hand side to hold the quill of the emu plume that spilled over the crown. We chose those plumes as carefully as any woman of the 1880s chose her ostrich plumes. And we wore them more flamboyantly, especially as we were more conscious of being out-of-date than glamorous. So we were not sorry when the horses were sent home and we made an immediate transmutation to an Armoured Corps with tracked Bren gun carriers instead of horses. But the army would not allow us to ride the carriers in our felt hats so we compromised by wearing the approved berets at an unapproved angle and teasing up strands from the centre stud till they formed a little pompon. The Armoured Corps lost its glamour when we found it was never to leave Australia. I transferred to the individualistic New Guinea Air Warning Wireless Company. Nobody worried what sort of hats we wore in that unit. Our only job was to get our messages through. For much of the time, anyway, I was attached to the American Fifth Air Force. We reported the movement of Japanese aircraft to American headquarters in Port Moresby.

Our three-man stations were scattered through Papua and New Guinea and on offshore islands. Those on the islands were placed there by barge, even by submarine. On the mainland we walked in, sometimes behind the Japanese lines, with a long line of native carriers bearing receiver, transmitter, wet-plate batteries, engine-driven battery-charger, petrol, oil, tools, weeks of food, coils of wire for aerials. It was our expertise with aerials that allowed the little AWA 3B sets to keep contact through jungles seemingly too thick for radio waves, over mountains impossibly high. And it was constant attention and good pidgin English that got our equipment in unbroken. The carriers worked in pairs with the loads slung on poles between them. After each hour's walking we stopped for a ten-minute break. The New Guinea way of putting a load down, even a trussed pig or cassowary, is with minimum effort. The front man steps forward, the rear man steps back, the load crashes between them. So at every stop we coaxed a gentle unloading. 'Ol

Hearing

boi harim gut! Na makim bokis i sindaun olsem lapun. Eesi nau! Eesi! Yu no lusim i bukarup pinis. Eesi!'

Pidgin is a musical and expressive language with beautifully tight vowels. It sounds absurd and childish if translated exactly into English: 'All boy hear good. Now make box it sit down all the same old man. Easy now. Easy. You not loose it it bugger up finish. Easy.'

But German with its compounded adjectives sounds preposterous if translated directly into English. So does Chinese with its out-of-place verbs and lack of articles. A young soldier in the Papuan Infantry Batallion from Manus Island told me of the girl he loved. He wanted to marry her but he did not know if she loved him. 'Love is elusive' he said. 'It cannot be taken.' The way he said it was: 'Mi no kisim win. I kam, i go, i no stap pinis.' 'Me no catch wind. He come, he go, he no stop finish.'

A spotter on an out-station reported aircraft sightings in plain language on a crystal-controlled emergency frequency to an always-tuned receiver at a sub-station. For months I helped man a sub-station at Gusap in the Ramu valley. We listened to Morse code from Port Moresby and the out-stations on one receiver, to the plain language reports on another. '4DX' a spotter would call, 'Seven Bettys south-east five thousand.' Before he had finished speaking I would begin sending the message by Morse code to Port Moresby: '4QG', our call-sign, 'O' for emergency, then the message. The signaller at head-quarters did not wait to acknowledge me. While he was writing down the last few words with his right hand, his left hand turned the handle that rang the telephone connected to the signals office at the American air-force. Information more than a minute old was of little use. From the time the spotter at Bena Bena saw seven Japanese Betty bombers flying south-east at five thousand feet to the time the American air-force was on full alert about twenty-five seconds would have elapsed. We were an efficient unit and a proud one.

Several former post-office employees joined us. They had operated sounders, the old telegraphic machines that sent Morse not as dots and dashes but as spaces between clicks. Click space click was a dash, click-click a dot. Under perfect conditions they could receive Morse code much quicker than

Celebration

any of us who had been trained in the army. All of them, even the youngest, carried their heads cocked a little to one side as though they were always listening, and since they had trained themselves to take telegrams even when serving customers, they had notable memories. One of them, on slack nights in the signals office, would continue playing poker while up to thirty four-figure cypher groups were sent, a full minute's transmission. Then he would get up calmly, walk across to the message pad, write down what had been sent, catch up to the operator and be ready to send R for received when the message ended. But none of them ever learnt to read through interference.

That was our specialty. We could follow a weak wavering signal through static, through whining carrier waves, through Morse signals from half a dozen other stations. One concentrated and deliberately tuned out all unwanted noises. A big Australian naval station, VNBR, interfered with us night and day. It was a few kilocycles off our frequency so we heard it not as pure signals but as hoarse blasts of air. When not transmitting messages the station played a tape to keep its channel open. For hour after hour we listened to our stations behind a repetition of VNBI VNBI VNBI DE (from) VNBR VNBR VNBR QTC NW QTC NW QTC NW (I have messages now) VNBI VNBI... After forty years those notes could still blot out my hearing if I let them.

Towards the end of our stay in Papua-New Guinea I was briefly in an Australian camp at Nadzab. I was walking back to my hut one night with two precious bottles of beer, a recent regular weekly issue. I passed the office of another signal group and heard the signaller on duty cursing interference. 'Oh Gawd! I can't get a bloody word.' I looked in the door, saw that I knew him, and said 'I'll clear your traffic while I drink my beer if you like.'

'No one could read that,' he said.

It is exciting concentrating till one is aware only of being ears. They worked shorter distances than we did but their radios were much smaller. The signals were very weak. Somewhere in the background my taste still functioned – I took a good swig of beer at the end of each message. But my ears felt bigger and distinct, as though they followed the faltering sound. They tracked it through other sounds, behind them, over them. When the second bottle of beer was finished the traffic was cleared. 'I always knew you thought you were good' said the signaller, 'but it never entered my head anyone could be that good. I can't read a word and all you've been sending is "Received. Send faster."'

Life in an American camp was a wonder. The food was so much better than ours and they cursed it so much more vehemently. We would sit down to a breakfast of tomato juice, flapjacks and maple syrup, bacon, eggs, toast with real butter, honey, coffee. The big flight-sergeant who usually sat opposite me would pick up his knife and fork, slice his pile of flapjacks in half, cut up his bacon and eggs, put down his knife, then take his fork in his right hand, spear half a flapjack and stuff it into his wide mouth. 'Back home' he would complain between chews, 'I wouldn't feed this goddamn shit to ma goddamn dawg.' He would spear a square of bacon and another half flapjack and sweep them through the pool of maple syrup. 'Jesus fuckin' Christ, I wouldn't!'

One of the sergeants in the aircraft maintenance section built a washing-machine out of a broken concrete mixer and a spare petrol engine. It worked so well he began doing the washing for his friends, too, and charging them for it. The officers began to patronise him so he built another washing machine and another. He spent much of every night washing for the whole camp. His commanding-officer called him up. He told him it was a valuable service he was doing. If he had more time could he do more washing? Well, yeah. Would he need more equipment? Well, yeah. Could he handle it all on his own? Well, hell, naw! He wasn't sleepin' too much as it was.

More concrete mixers and engines were flown in. He was detached from duties so he could work in the daytime, so were two or three of his buddies. Distant units flew washing to him. A regular service by air developed. He paid his offsiders. All of them continued to draw their pay while they ran a private laundry for profit with army equipment and army fuel. I passed him one day while he was adding up figures. 'Holy shit!' he said. 'It's a beautiful war.'

The Americans could pull into a patch of heavy jungle

Celebration

in a morning, clear it, erect tents, mess hall, kitchen, offices, dig latrines, lay on telephone and electric light, and have an open-air screen with seating for several hundred ready to show pictures the same night. We saw newsreels denied to civilians by the censors: the German bombing of England, the British bombing of Germany, aerial dogfights, hand-to hand jungle fighting, tank clashes in the Libyan desert. It was fascinating because it was a record of what happened, not propaganda. The men with the cameras stood beside the men with the guns or rode with them in the bombers and fighters.

We saw the latest American films. Sometimes a film was released in the New Guinea jungle before it was released in New York. Fred Astaire and Ginger Rogers danced miraculously in stories that could not even begin to cope with a miracle. Bette Davis acted in stories so carefully chosen her work is timeless. Rita Hayworth and Betty Grable and other long-legged blondes danced and sang their way through films never intended to be anything but froth and flesh. And always there were stories of more flesh than we saw. 'Man, that dame! She never wore no panties. You know that scene where she's bein' carried toward the camera, legs apart. Well that there scene had to be retook. The director, he sent her back to put her panties on. But that first take, the cameraman he filmed it right to the end, and he run off some stills. Look! Ah got one, right here!'

The American khaki work-suit, or zoot suit, had many pockets. The inside left pocket was reserved for photographs of girl friend or wife and children – 'Ah keep 'em right here, right next to ma heart'. The convenient outside top right-hand pocket was reserved for the collection of pornography. And genuine or faked, that photograph was the plum of most collections. 'She never wore no panties nowhere. She was in a night-club, three parts stewed and gettin' randy. So her boy-frien', he jist turned 'er on 'er ass across the table, an' he chawed it like a cob o' corn.' The extra stories added piquancy to what was after all a dark and distant cunt.

During filming one night in Port Moresby a red alert sounded. Japanese aircraft had been sighted. Two huge Negro transport drivers rose like jack-in-the-boxes from the

Hearing

front row, took five or six great leaps towards the screen, and dived through it to the slit trench they knew was immediately behind. Someone stitched the screen together. The all clear sounded. The scattered audience returned. The red alert sounded again. The two Negroes took the same short path to the trench.

The Americans were generally more excitable than Australians. During an unexpected red alert at Gusap most ran for the trenches so quickly they forgot to turn the lights off in the tents. The whole camp blazed an invitation to the bombers. So those who had taken their machine-guns to the trenches shot the lights out. Bullets screamed through the camp from all angles. I flattened myself in the bottom of my trench, scrabbling like a Spiny Anteater to get deeper. My head felt as fragile and as exposed as a light bulb.

Our job was the reporting of Japanese troop movement as well as aircraft. Once the Japanese knew where one of our stations was its job was over. It had to move elsewhere if it could get out. So we did little fighting. I was shot at only once during four years in the army. A sniper fired three shots at me as I walked along a native track. It is an unreal experience. One feels incredulous, angry, afraid. The bullets seem to be live things. They hiss going past, or do they sigh? One wonders absurdly whether they threaten or regret missing. Then one leaps for cover.

On Bougainville in the Solomon Islands, where I spent the last few months of the war, a big field gun fired at our camp for six nights. We dug our slit trench in our tent. We stepped out of bed into it. It was half full of water and impossible to drain. Bougainville is wet. We crouched with our noses almost in the water. The shell that brought us out of bed the first night landed short. Two more exploded short. The next one must land on us. We held our breath and sank lower into the water. The next shell was long. Two more were long. The seventh shell must land in between. Now they had the range for sure. We could not hold our breath any longer. We crouched and shivered. Would we hear the seventh or just explode with it? It never came. And so it was for the next five nights: three shells short, three long. Then our infantry found the gun.

The war ended while we were on Bougainville. Liberator

Celebration

bombers took us back to Australia. I boarded one with twenty-odd others on the strip of white crushed coral at Torokina. The pilot explained that without a bomb load passengers unbalanced the plane for take-off. Twelve men must stand in the bomb bay. We seemed to be more than halfway down the strip when his urgent voice came over the intercom, 'More in the bomb bay! More in the bomb bay! She won't lift!' He had not noticed how thin we all were. So those of us nearest pressed hurriedly along the narrow beam where the downward-swinging doors met. We grasped the waist of the man in front and we pushed him forward hoping enough were coming in behind to make up the weight. The doors looked so frail we felt if we stumbled and fell on them they would drop us through. Though there was nowhere to fall. The doors seemed to be imperfectly closed and two white ribbons of coral three centimetres wide raced under us much too close. The plane did not seem to be lifting at all. Then we saw green leaves under us, closer even than the ground had been. We cleared the jungle by centimetres. When we saw water below us and felt the plane level off, we backed out warily and sat on the floor in the tail section. There were no seats. What did that matter? We were going home. I was going home to write.

I went back to farming because I loved it. I wrote poetry because I loved it and it was a greater experience writing one's own than reading it. One examined something with one's imagination. All five senses focussed on it till one saw it better than it had ever been seen. Then one found the words to keep it. Something new was set in music.

The blaze of understanding that makes a poem is a sometimes thing. It cannot be conjured up; it can be maintained when it comes. But it comes at inconvenient times, even pushing itself disconcertingly through other writing, and unless it is welcomed and worked on immediately, it disappears. I did not want to write only in flashes. I wanted something that would engross all my intelligence for years at a time. I thought of novels. I tried short stories. It took me twenty years to find what I could do: write non-fiction as intensely as a poem. Each scene had to live, each word justify itself. The English language is precise. Usually one word only fits perfectly. That gives meaning. The phrasing, the patterning of exact words makes the meaning memorable. Each page must be a seam of opal, not a slice of suet pudding.

I decided to answer a question that had fascinated me since boyhood: where did Australia's imported animals come from? Who brought in the first rabbit, the first fox, the first sparrow? What was said about them when they began to breed? Why did they breed so prolifically? The questioning had intensified unobtrusively. The book demanded to be written. It seemed the reason for my existence. I went to the Mitchell Library to see what information there was. I spent two weeks sampling the listings in the catalogues, in searching old newspapers. Information was there. The book could be written. The information was scattered but it was retrievable and exciting. The search would absorb me for years. I found newspaper references could be confirmed through parliamentary debates, government gazettes, land office documents, papers of acclimatisation societies, royal commissions. Newspaper research in the 1960s was beneath the dignity of serious historians. It brought them too close to emotional people and too far away from unemotional facts. I wanted people in my story. They had brought in the animals. They had lived with them when they prospered unbelievably. I counted up how many newspapers were extant that might have information about rabbits – about seven thousand. I would read the lot. And perhaps stories about wild donkeys and horses and hares would turn up as a bonus.

'Do you mean to tell me' said one historian, 'that you are going to sit there going through newspaper after newspaper, that you don't know whether there's anything in them, that you don't even know what you are looking for, that you are just going to look? You can't write a history that way.'

I wrote to A. H. Chisholm, the ornithologist who had edited the *Australian Encyclopaedia*. He told me he had had the same idea forty-five years before me. The information was so diffuse no man could collect it.

But apart from the massive job of research, it is not easy switching from being a poet and a farmer (I had no doubt about which order they came in) to a full-time writer with a farm. It is not a logical step. Uneasy friends ask how much money is in it when all one is certain of is the cost of paying good labour to do one's work on the farm for five or six years plus the cost of months at a time at libraries in several cities and thousands of kilometres of travel by car around the country and by Land-Rover into the central deserts. My mother told me it was grossly unfair to leave a wife and young children to manage alone. Leave the book until the children were older. That seemed a demand to stop breathing for years. Friends who read a lot asked 'But even if you write the book who'll read it? The subject hasn't got general interest.'

I knew the book would be published. Douglas Stewart at Angus and Robertson was waiting for it. I was certain the time was right. Just as much as talent an author has to have an awareness of his audience. No quality of writing can save a book that is too soon or too late. Interest in Australia was obviously increasing in the 1960s. A book that explained the Australian landscape would sell. I went to a writers' week in Adelaide – it might have been the first held – to bolster my courage. How did other writers order their lives?

The trip seemed to be disheartening. Most writers worked at night after they got home from work, or else they got up early and wrote for two or three hours before they went to work. Four or five years full-time on one book was something they had never thought of. It was a luxury unavailable to Australian authors unless one was a wealthy dilettante. They thought I was lucky to have a farm. So I was. But it was a small farm. We had no reserves to draw on. I had to manage it, even from a distance, without an error for the next several years or book and farm would crash. Was it possible?

On the second last night of writers' week most of us went to a party – I do not even remember where. At the end, twenty or thirty waited outside on the footpath for ordered taxis to take us to various hotels and motels. My taxi pulled up and I walked towards it. Big Olaf Ruhen, the first Australian writer to be accepted consistently by American magazines, called to the taxi-driver above the heads of those still waiting 'Look after that man! He's important.'

Hearing

He had no more than a short story and poems in several magazines to go by. So with full confidence I began work on *They All Ran Wild* in the South Australian Archives the next morning. And for the next four years, for the first time in my life, all my energies concentrated on building something that was worth building. I knew why I was alive. And the life of the whole family grew richer, even if more difficult. Our days were unexpected.

Lecturing is an offshoot of writing. It is a distraction. From the time I am asked to give a lecture until the time I am on my feet – sometimes twelve months – I am uneasy. One is so much aware one has to be good. One has to put one's being on show, not just one's words. So I do not give many lectures. But a writer has to keep in contact with people. He gets his words from God-knows-where and he gets them only when he is alone. He gets his inspiration from people.

It is exciting playing on an audience. One speaks to them all but occasionally one picks out individuals and speaks to them, watching for response. It is especially exciting when the audience is big. One hears the murmurs of astonishment. Laughter from five hundred has so much more satisfying volume than laughter from five. It is good to make statements and hear them quoted. Every lecture should have something original in it worth quoting. Why quote from somebody else? That merely shows one can read.

'Speed reading is a good thing for the quick getting of facts. But I don't want my books gobbled up at two to three thousand words a minute. It would be supplying *pâté de foie gras* for a pie-eating contest...'

'I like to declare emphatically that this is the best time anyone could have been alive. But I know that is not true. Every man who has loved life has believed that of his age...'

I used those sentences in a long lecture that excited me and excited several hundred English teachers. One man asked me afterwards if I thought it possible for an ordinary man to develop my philosophy. I said 'Yes, if he was brave enough.'

In Adelaide, it must have been about the end of the 1960s, I gave a talk against censorship. That is not long ago but our reading was still closely supervised by the prurient

Celebration

Minister for Customs. I had been in Adelaide for weeks giving a series of lectures to city and country schools and at the University of Adelaide. I was being paid well by the university. I also held a Commonwealth Literary Fund fellowship. I had recently had four banned books sent to me from England: Steven Marcus's *The Other Victorians*, Philip Roth's *Portnoy's Complaint*, John Cleland's *Fanny Hill*, and Hubert Selby Junior's *Last Exit to Brooklyn*, first published in 1957 and denied to Australians twelve years later. The elderly friend who sent them found England was not as enlightened about books as I thought. Perhaps they were freely available in London. In the big county bookshops where he first tried, shopgirls said 'Not likely!' or 'Cor! At your age!'

So someone suggested that since I was being doubly paid by the government, and since I held four illegal books, I ought to use them to talk about the censorship that harassed everyone who thought.

I began, unusually for me and only since I had faith in the quality of what I was to say, with a quote from another author: Christina Stead's brilliant observation in *For Love Alone*.

' "Everyone likes the obscene; that is real life" said Teresa, the bare-boned girl unexpectedly, opening her lips for the first time.

"Not a great artist" stormed Clara.

"Those more than the others because their violence is more" said Teresa.'

Five nuns sat in the front row. I spoke to convince them. Since quoting from the books was one of the aims of the talk, I finished with an appalling sentence of Selby's, nearly two thousand words long, describing not the pack rape, the public fucking of Tralala. It presents the viciousness of animals, people or poultry, confined in cramped spaces.

At the end of the talk one of the nuns came to me immediately. Her eyes glittered, her cheeks were flushed, beads of sweat hung on her top lip. 'That was marvellous' she said, 'like a scene from the Divine Comedy modernised. I'm the Mother Superior of a girls' school. I need to know about life. Such books should not be censored.' She troub-

Hearing

led me deeply. She had the energy to meet life physically, not merely psychically in books.

Before *The River* was published I sent typescripts to a class of intelligent twelve-year-olds to see how they liked it. Children often pick up weaknesses that adults miss. That book follows our sometimes difficult life on the Namoi River so accurately I did not change the names of any of the family. They are all in it as they were, their dogs and their ponies. One boy wrote 'This book tells what a fairytale life on a farm would be like'. I had never felt so lucky. Now that luck has been confirmed over and over. One writes one's way into Wonderland.

Touch and Feelings

A bed without a welcoming bare bum in it is no more than half a bed, a place to sleep in, not to wonder in. We sleep linked together, a nipple, usually erected, studded into a palm, penis, usually erected, denting a buttock or cushioned between the outer lips of her vulva. She seems more conscious of breaking apart than I. At intervals during the night I hear 'Give me a cuddle'. Our bodies respond immediately. We hook together and fall to sleep again in seconds. What flows between us in those brief moments of waking: warmth immediately, gratitude, energy, respect, comfort, interest, wonder, excitement, trust, curiosity, expectation, need, relief, lust? Added together, I suppose, they simply make love.

Sometimes we reverse the position. Her pubes warm my buttocks. There is no better cure for a cold bum than a poultice of cunt and curly hair. Crisp hairs stroke as she breathes. My buttocks tingle. As a bonus she moves a little more and winks her vulva – an exquisite chewing.

When we lived on the river the water closet was outside so she pissed on the lawn in the early morning. She would slide across me back into bed, cunt as cold as a dog's nose. 'Warm my feet!'

'Jesus! They're all frosty. Didn't you put any shoes on?'

'I was in a hurry.'

The urgency increased when she was pregnant. She had quick, shallow orgasms then, too, as though her body gave her as much relief as it could without disturbing the baby.

Her getting out of bed on a summer's morning is a delight. She slides to the bed edge, puts her feet to the floor. As she straightens a brown tassel of pubic hair blooms suddenly between her widely-spaced thighs, then disappears. She dresses quickly. I think of it as the morning bud-burst. She is unconscious of it.

Touch and feelings

I wrote a poem about her going to bed. It reads simply but it took years to get right and I finished it only three or four years ago. I read it at the Talking Book of the Year Award at the Royal Blind Society in Sydney in 1981. Barbara Blackman came to her and said 'How did you like being exposed in public? I was exposed for twenty years as an artist's wife. Isn't it wonderful?'

Meg Going to Bed

She undresses unconsciously although she knows I watch her.
She ignores the sleeve turned inside out on her jumper
Like a child hurrying into bed.

The gay blouse I bought her may crumple on a chair back.
She reaches to undo the hooked elastic on her bare back
And stoops to drop her breasts free.

They swing as she straightens. Cold stiffens the nipples.
The areolae stained in pregnancy are bronze as apples.
She scratches where the cups rubbed

And huddles into a pyjama coat as shapeless as love.
She balances each foot athletically to remove
Shoes, socks and jeans.

She strips off her panties, teases her pubic hair,
Picks up the pyjama pants she decides not to wear
And drops them at the foot of the bed.

Then she crawls towards her pillow. Her coat rides out of reach
Of her buttocks and displays her cushiony arch
Framed between her thighs.

She curls under the blankets, picks up yesterday's newspaper
And props herself lightly on her side. But, a sudden sleeper,
She soon lies among crumpled pages.

And when I join her, awake or asleep
She moves to welcome me, if I am not too cold, and I keep
Aware of her integrity.

Celebration.

Lovemaking commits the senses as nothing else commits them, especially the sense of touch. As hands fondle with varying contact, wonder at the texture of flesh comes up through palms and fingertips. There was once a blind judge of Hereford cattle in New South Wales. His hands not only told him the conformation of the beasts, they showed him the lovely coat pattern of white on red as clearly as eyes. He could pick up one faulty red splotch in the white blaze on a nose. In lovemaking seeing enhances touch but the deeper appreciation comes through the hands. Flat hands feel the firm, flat belly. Fingertips trace the little knot sunken in the niche of the navel. Shoulder blades and forehead do not yield – one is aware of bone. The inside of thighs are delicate and smooth, chest corrugated. The calves of the legs show the strength of flesh. It resists, pulls away. Breasts and buttocks are plastic. Whole hands fill with flesh, fingers sink into it. But it will not be moulded. It springs instantly back to shape. Thumb and forefinger trace the solid crinkly little columns of nipples. Finger-tips rise and fall over rippled areolae. Lips feel lush and tickle the fingers lightly as fingers tickle them. There is soft short hair, and soft long hair that draws so lightly through the fingers it seems to whisper to them, crisp hair, harsh hair, hair like down, two or three long, single coarse hairs that roll underneath the fingers across the flesh. The vulva at first is no special flesh. The pubic hair excites the hands: elastic coils, straight ridges and spreading tufts. But the vulva enjoys the fingers. It acknowledges them. It moves, yields, grows spongy and firm, soft and slimy, deep and slippery, grooved, seamed, open and closed. Each part feels different.

Then one realises that as one strokes one is stroked. Flesh feels through flesh. One is no longer aware of two bodies. All one's faculties become feeling. Penis and vulva magnify them and direct them in a great glow towards some peak that seems always unattainable. How can pleasure so exquisite increase? No matter how often it is reached, until it is reached it seems unreachable, an impossible peak. When my penis is quiescent I regard it with amazement – such a little cylinder of flesh and it brings pleasure that remains unbelievable. And its chief wonder, what makes one regard

Touch and feelings

it with the utmost kindness, is the more pleasure it gives the more it takes.

I was born before men and women could masturbate happily. I grew up between two schools, the one that said masturbation would send you mad and the doubtfully more enlightened school that reckoned it merely an unmanly pastime that was better sublimated in hard work. Luckily my penis ignored all advice. It simply made demands that were irrepressible.

My most lasting memory of adolescence and young manhood is of an erect penis. I did an enormous amount of study – I learnt to get information fast and to coordinate it, although I had no idea then what I could do with it. My penis was a constant and fascinating interruption. The harder I worked, the stiffer it rose.

It poked holes in my underpants. I would sit in a tram. Vibrations from the wheels travelled through the seat, through my buttocks into my groin. Any movement excited it. I would feel the head nudging against an unmended hole. I would try not to think about it. That aggravated it. The head prodded harder, broke through the hole and snared itself like a Bearded Dragon lizard in wire-netting. I would will it to subside so it could extricate itself. Concern for it caused more engorgement. The corona flared over the hole. Good God! It would cut off the return of blood and go gangrenous, a genuine fear. It seemed prepared to hold its head up throbbing for hours. The clear, miraculously slippery, cleansing and lubricating fluid would begin to ooze out of it. It came up in beads. I could feel every millimetre of the progress. Before it choked its head off, it would have time to soak a shameful great patch in the front of my trousers. I would watch from the tram for a hotel with a side-entrance to its lavatory – I was too young to go through the bar – then leap off at the next stop, subdue the penis and release it.

When very young I deduced that the idea of sublimation was an absurdity. Why did we see that our rams and bulls did not get overfat and lazy? Good health meant good sex. Anyway, the feelings usually preceded the thoughts. The penis itself projected erotic visions on a screen behind my

Celebration

eyes. It had automatic control as well as conscious control that worked the on switch only. With penis switched off the screen was blank. I could work freely. Switched on, it moved naked figures about so enticingly I had to take notice of it.

But whenever the handful of clotted slime was disposed of somewhere, and the dispirited remnant, drooling a little, was tucked back inside the underpants, there was always a sense of unease. Rationalisation did not completely triumph over conditioning. In the 1980s there are two divisions of English-speaking people: those born before happy masturbation, those born after. But appallingly, some out-of-date counsellors are still in positions of influence. At a college for Aboriginal boys in Darwin, students who by tribal law will be kept apart from women until they are at least twenty-four years old are told that masturbation is evil. 'God will not love you if you do such terrible things to your bodies.'

Some men declare proudly that their intellect rules their passion. I doubt their passion, doubt their intellects. Mental energy stems from physical energy. Without my balls I would have less brains. In any case why be proud of subduing the greatest marvel of being alive?

Even now, when I am away alone on research, sex interrupts me as it interrupted my school days. I work in five to six week stretches and I work to the limit of my physical capacity: eight to nine hours fast reading and note-taking a day, seven days a week. Research is much more than gathering information. One has to build the book as one goes. The information decides the chapters, the length of the book. Each new piece of information has to fit somewhere or else one takes notes that are unnecessary or misses notes that are necessary. It is exciting work. Australian history is so diffuse and so hidden among illogical records one discovers a new country. One cannot go into anything with preconceived ideas. And popular conceptions of Australia are mostly wrong.

After a few days on one's own whiskers grow more quickly. Then the skin on one's chest becomes sensitive. Where the shirt touches it teases. One smells stronger and wonders if it can be noticed. Does one advertise one is in rut? After a month one opens a book in the library and all one can see is cunt. It covers the page. One has to part the lips to read

Touch and feelings

behind them. Masturbation makes no difference. When the penis flags desire does not. It seems as much spiritual as physical. After six weeks I see everything through a red mist. It is clearly time to go home.

I cannot take sex casually. It is the deepest communication two people can have. One fondles with one's whole being. Careless lovemaking betrays oneself. Though with the right partner it ought to be carefree. It is much too serious to be taken too seriously.

What does one ejaculate? A common concept is power. I spout gratitude, I think. You have brought me to the fittest celebration of being alive. Here, this is how I thank you.

The ultimate experience is answering the cry 'I want another baby'. One tries to time the orgasms, man first, woman shortly after, so that there is a pool of semen for the cervix to suck up. And what does it matter if one mistimes? It is just as good trying again. Control improves the performance as in writing poetry. Imagination responds to discipline. Obstacles challenge it.

Havelock Ellis in his triumphant and originative *Studies in the Psychology of Sex* emphasises the vitality of the womb: 'The uterus becomes shorter, broader, and softer during the orgasm, at the same time descending lower into the pelvis, with its mouth open intermittently, so that, as one writer remarks, spontaneously recurring to the simile which commended itself to the Greeks, "the uterus might be likened to an animal gasping for breath".'

If the womb reaches for the semen, the vagina actively welcomes the penis. One is conscious, not of thrusting, but of being drawn in. Glowing flesh pulsates about the penis, enfolds it, yields to it. It responds to every movement, and at the time of orgasm the vulva grasps the base of the penis while the vagina first ripples over it then squeezes it rhythmically with diminishing force and at lengthening intervals. Joan never acknowledged her body's astonishing capacity. She liked something to squeeze on during orgasm and her body's response to it was no more than she expected. Anyway, she was unconvinced all bodies did not respond as enthusiastically.

The eighteenth-century girls in John Cleland's *Fanny Hill* did not receive their lovers as simply as modern women.

Celebration

Cleland, as vague about female anatomy as most modern pornographers, seemed to think girls were equipped, not only with hymens, but with vaginas that were sealed for the full length like stuck-together sausage casings. So their first lovers with penises built like battering-rams had not only to lunge through a barred door but batter their way down the length of the hall. Louisa one day, noticing that her finger 'was something of the shape of what I pined for' threw herself on her bed and 'with great agitation and delight did I deflower myself as far as it could reach'. Fanny herself in her first experience with Charles had to cram her petticoat in her mouth to stifle her screams. And that was after his 'machine driving forward with fury at the slit breaks the union of those parts'. He rested there 'lip-deep' but then 'he improved his advantage, and following well his stroke in a straight line, forcibly deepens his penetration; but put me to such intolerable pain, from the separation of the sides of that soft passage by a hard thick body, I could have scream'd out'. Even a later lover with a bigger penis spent time 'winning his way inch by inch'.

When the orgasms were over and we lay together slack, complete, as normal as one ever can be, I marvelled sometimes at the struggle going on inside her. The tangible experiences were over. Now in silence and in darkness spermatozoa raced for the glory of existence. One among hundreds of millions would win. And the event made less impression than a collision of stars in the outer universe.

The arena was prepared remarkably. A usually hostile, acid field was smeared with a kind alkaline fluid deep enough for spermatazoa to swim in. Nurtured in the testicles as inert invisible elements they were suddenly expelled into a mixture of fluids that animated them and protected them as they were ejected with it into the arena as live things with tails lashing. Have they a course to follow like migrating birds or do they thrash about aimlessly? Do they jostle one another? Are they aware of their incompleteness? Do they strive harder as they near the ovum? How many hundred thousand vie over the last quarter of a centimetre? And when the ovum receives the first to butt against it, by what fraction of a second has it won? Do the losers then stub

Touch and feelings

themselves to death against a sealed wall? If no ovum is ready, if there is a delay of many hours, do those first at the site lose momentum and die, and another, perhaps from the vestibule of the vulva, find its way through the dead and the dying and succeed? The meeting is momentous, yet no female animal is aware of it. Life forms as insignificantly as a crystal of snow.

The main difference between humans and other animals seems to be not in their intellectual abilities (dolphins might well be our equals) but in their lovemaking. Ours is a spiritual need as much as a physical need. So lovemaking continues through pregnancy and through those years when pregnancy is not wanted. For thousands of years the search for a good contraceptive has been unsuccessful.

The country doctor who fitted Joan with her first diaphragm inserted one that was too big, lost control of it and let it flip open. She was sore for a fortnight. They were undignified and unspontaneous things to use. The woman had to coat it with spermicide, lie on her back, fold it, insert it, allow it to open gently, press it around wherever her cervix seemed to be, follow it with an applicator full of spermicide, wash the applicator and her hands, then leap into bed randy. Her cunt no longer smelt excitingly of cunt, it smelt like a perfume bar in a chain store. It was unkissable.

After one of the spermicides blistered my penis – luckily it did not affect her – we decided they were unlovable in any form. A very modern gynaecologist fitted her with a Lippes loop, an S-shaped plastic device with an extra squiggle on the end, that fitted into the womb and mysteriously interfered with its function. It gave her cramps. She smelt of stale blood. She bore it for three weeks. I found her one night sitting naked on a kitchen chair groping for the threads that told her the device was in place. She was crying, a rare occurrence. 'I don't feel like me. It hurts and I smell and I hate it. Pull it out!' She had about one centimetre of one thread on show.

I clamped it between thumb and forefinger and pulled gingerly. 'Are you sure it's safe just to pull these things out? Shouldn't your cervix be dilated before it's taken out?

'I don't know. Just pull!'

Celebration

So I pulled. The doctor was five hundred kilometres away. One could not pull on it with the confidence and the experience of a fishing line. God knows what would come out on the end of it.

'Keep on pulling!' It astonished me how hard I had to pull. 'It isn't hurting. Pull!'

So I pulled; it gave way; it came out, a nasty-looking thing with clots of blood in every loop. She threw it out, kissed me, and went to bed. 'I'll be right in the morning.'

The doctors we knew prescribed the new contraceptive pills for their patients and cautioned their wives against using them. Condoms had been used for hundreds of years, made first of oiled linen, then of sheep gut. Casanova remarked he was not going to 'shut myself up in a piece of dead skin to prove that I am perfectly alive'. He offered his women half a squeezed lemon as a cervical cap. Even the modern thin rubber condoms earned the reputation that 'A fuck with a frenchy is as good as a shower with a raincoat on'.

So, since a fourth pregnancy would have been inconvenience, not disaster, we practised the oldest and freest contraceptive method: withdrawal, or 'getting off at Redfern' in the imaginative Australian vernacular. Redfern was the last stop before the old railway terminus at Central Station, Sydney. And perhaps again, discipline enhanced lovemaking. We worked towards her orgasm first, whether quick or slow. And the ejaculating penis was a new spectacle. It had usually fired into warm darkness. Sometimes she felt it, often she did not. When a woman has had her orgasm, the whole vagina is fairly insensitive. During orgasm she can be aware of nothing but release. In the build-up to orgasm the little mound in the front wall of the vagina called the Grafenberg spot is alive. It is as susceptible as the clitoris. It aches to be stroked and the penis strokes it best. But as she nears orgasm the firm mouth of the cervix softens, grows sensitive and receptive. Before it begins to suck during orgasm, it can record semen squirting against it.

She had had her orgasm. Penis, about to shoot, pointed away from her face. The first surge, usually the strongest, merely oozed on to her left breast. So it relaxed, did not worry about direction. A sudden unaimed jet caught her

Touch and feelings

beneath the chin. 'Almost a bulls-eye' she said happily. 'Have you got a handkerchief?'

Once, sensing my orgasm, she pulled away, and with a most unaccustomed lascivious look on her face, watched it squirt on to her belly. I seemed to be watching a different woman. Then she easily had her orgasm. 'Have you got a handkerchief?' After the orgasm comes not sadness, but practicality. And the vulva that before orgasm was shy and elusive is relaxed and uncaring.

In summer mopping up is cursory. Semen dries quickly. In winter no amount of mopping up is successful. It has no power of retaining heat. Within seconds top sheet, bottom sheet, thighs, buttocks, belly, chest, pubic hair are spattered with sorbet of semen. Mop up quickly what can be found, then lie unmoving, too sleepy to seek out the remaining frozen flakes, unwilling to touch what the flesh will shrink from.

How many women scorn the missionary position in the winter? It is the bum on top that has to waggle in the cold. I can get my hands round hers to massage it and warm it. She cannot reach mine. But anyway, she finds it luxurious on the bottom being warmed at once from outside and in.

On the morning of my father's funeral I woke to the question 'Would it be awful to do it this morning?' It is the best start to any day. On the day of a funeral it carries assurance as a bonus.

We were supposed to travel with my mother in a line of huge black cars with black-clad chauffeurs. It looked like an articulated ferry between life and death. We led my mother to our dusty Peugeot and drove among the mourning cars secure in this world. Dürer's *Hands* was reproduced on the wall of the chapel in the crematorium. I would rather have had Gulley Jimson's *Feet*. At the end of the service the undertaker came to say goodbye. He was an undertaker's caricature, a long man in a long black suit with a long yellow face set in professional gloom. His voice had a hollow ring to it as though he practised his words in a vault. He held out his hand to be shaken and I absentmindedly shook it. It was graveyard damp. I wanted to wash. We did it again that night as reassurance. My teeth were on edge.

Cattle parade about a dead beast. We had forty-two crossbred Santa Gertrudis heifers in a lucerne paddock. One

Celebration

bloated. Gases form in the paunch, blow a plug of chewed leaves into the oesophagus when the animal belches, then gas formation accelerates. The animal swells till air gets into the bloodstream and it dies in minutes. The dead heifer was a parody of the dead. She lay on her back with four grotesque legs poked up stiffly like leaning pillars. They were more than twice the thickness of ordinary legs. The hooves could not swell so the skin had bulged round them till they were almost hidden. The belly was drum tight and enormous, eyes popping. The huge tongue protruded between lips that were rolls of blubber. Anus and genitals were elephantine. Even the long thin delicate tail was now a massive roll with a tassel on the end.

The other heifers fed uneasily for an hour or so but they kept looking at the dead heifer and above her. Deep red and black, long-legged, short-haired, they were beautiful animals with loose roomy skin and alert eyes. They stepped as cleanly as fillies. Their ancestors had been bred to draw carriages.

At last they all came together and walked in slow single file to the dead one. They circled her, stopped, turned inward, watched her for a while and watched above her, then they began to pace round her. Mouths opened and they mooed quietly. Streams of heavy saliva slipped off their tongues and floated like silver ribbons holding them to the circle. They quickened the pacing, began to trot. Now and again one or two keened on a long high note. Dust rose, settled across the dead one like a pall. One broke the circle, trotted to the dead beast, flopped on her knees and stretched her chin across its body. She bellowed and stroked it with her chin. Ropes of saliva fell from her mouth. She got up, looked at the body, looked upward, then resumed pacing. Another heifer ran in and another. Twelve or more at a time approached from different angles and caressed the body with chins and necks. It grew wet with saliva. As one rose bellowing and rejoined the circle another took its place. The scene grew vague with dust. Presently they all came back into the circle. They steadied down, moaning softly. All still watched the body and sometimes looked up. Then they drifted out individually to feed.

But for the next hour or so they were watchful. What do

Touch and feelings

they see or fear to see or hope to see? They worried me. They were displaying no beast-like complacency with life or death. I tried to write a poem about it but could never get it right. Then one night I heard Les Murray read a poem about a ceremony he had seen. He did get his poem right. And it astonished me since few people have seen such a full ceremony. Most cattle just gallop up to a dead beast, mill round it bellowing and dribbling, then gallop away in confusion.

For centuries people have reported the dancing of hares. I have never seen it though I watch for it. Sometimes I have seen a hare stand up and kick about a bit as though it could dance, but nothing more. The few that have seen the dance tell of hares meeting in pairs. They stand facing one another, forepaws touching, and kick sideways in unison, a quick rhythmic movement. They circle kicking, leap in the air, break, spin round and meet again.

Brolgas, big Australian cranes, meet in flocks of up to forty to dance. There are few left anywhere in southern Australia, and their opportunistic feeding migrations have been upset by farming and imported animals in northern Australia. The dance is one of the world's wonders. I watched about fifteen birds briefly from a train window one morning years ago. They usually begin dancing in pairs. Birds bow to each other, fold wings in front of the body, hold wings outstretched and entwine necks, move apart, together, sidle, stretch left wing to meet the partner's right wing, then the other wing, both wings together. They circle together, break apart, bow, circle separately. Then in the same rhythm the flock dances into two opposing lines. They approach each other, stepping long and pointing the feet, trailing the wings on the ground, spreading them. They pass one another with wings folded, turn, repeat the movement.

Some routines are complicated. They seem to be dances that the flock has learnt. Lines of birds face one another, step three paces to one side, three paces back the other way, two paces to one side, two paces back. They run together, all turn the one way and circle, leaping into the air and down again lightly every third step. If a bird makes a mistake and throws a movement into confusion, those nearest peck it back into line.

The soil keeps a man in perspective. It gives him as much

Celebration

as he can wonder at. He gives it as much as he can learn. It confutes him so easily. Look at the plants germinating in a paddock. Run one's fingers through the soil. Feel its temperature, its texture. One can judge what crops it will grow best. Is the paddock too wet to sow? Does the soil rake easily through the fingers or does it cake in muddy lumps? Is it too dry to sow? Take a handful from sowing depth, squeeze it into a ball, throw it thirty centimetres high and let it fall back into the palm. If it does not crumble on the fourth throw seeds will germinate. How deep is the moisture? Is there sustenance for the roots that will travel over a metre deep? Dig down with shovel or auger.

One looks at the seeds that are to be sown, picks up a half handful, weighs it in the palm. Is it the right weight for that seed? One can estimate very accurately. Light seeds might not germinate well. Are there any damaged seeds? What percentage? Are there weed seeds? Trickle seeds from one hand to the other. Spread samples on the palm. Push them about with a finger.

So one sows. A storm not forecast can flood the paddock two days later and rot the seed. There might be no rain to follow. The seed germinates, persists for weeks, dies. As soon as it has died, the rains come. The crop can grow vigorously, begin to flower. An extraordinary late frost, a new disease, can turn it into mush.

One works by the feel of the soil, knowing one never has more than a part of the story. One can never be confident. One always has to do more than enough. Contact with the soil is especially good for a writer. It preserves his essential sense of the ridiculous. Some years one can look back with considerable self-mockery and realise that if one had done nothing at all one would be much better off.

But then there are the years when the stock are fat in the paddock and grains are fat in the head. We rock our fingers over the backbones in the lambs' loins appreciating flesh and fat. We catch their tails, hold the woolly top with the thumb and knead the bare under-side with four fingers feeling for bone and depth of fat.

Wheat is thrashed between the hands. Crush a rough, awned head with the heel of one hand grinding it into the palm of the other. From harvest to harvest one never forgets that feel, the first test of the crop. The husked grains have to be ground out of the head, the seed out of the husk. Then hold the palm out, blow gently. Some awn, husk and stalk blow away. Splintered awns are stuck into the palm. Pull them out. Shake the grain up. Blow again. Count the grains. Count the grains in a number of heads picked at random. Count the heads in sixty-centimetre sections of rows. A formula I have never fully converted to metrics gives me the yield: twenty-six grains in each sixty centimetres of rows eighteen centimetres apart make one bushel to the acre.

What of the quality of the grain? How heavy is it? Are there any pink grains, any brown or purple or red diseased tips? Bite it. What is the protein content? Barley should be a plump, soft grain, white and floury inside. Wheat should be almost too hard to chew and such a light amber colour it seems translucent. Chew a dozen grains. Swallow the starch with the saliva. A wad of gluten bigger than a stick of chewing gum should be left in the mouth. One regards it with satisfaction. All one knows has gone into growing the crop.

With the first header I ever owned, towed and driven by a little, kerosene-fueled tractor, I stripped a crop of wheat infested with black oats. The wheat was a variety that was hairy and prickly. The black oats were hairier and pricklier. The temperature was up to 48°C by day; at night it did not drop below 38°C. The tractor had no cabin, no canopy, its little iron seat was unsprung. Pimples formed on my sweat-soaked buttocks. I would sit to one side, to the other, square on the seat. Every position was painful. I sat there for twelve hours a day. A constant light wind picked up the dust and chaff from the back of the header and blew it over me down one long side of the paddock. Waist, the back of my neck, wrists, under the arms, inside the elbows, behind the knees, eyes itched and prickled till they felt on fire. Tears ran down my cheeks in muddy streams. My lips cracked and pained. Along the other three sides I wiped the hairy dust from inside my joints, mopped my eyes, cooled down a little, then turned the corner to be tortured again. Sometimes black oats and pieces of straw blocked the revolving screen that conducted the grain into the box. I had to climb on to the header, and reach in with one hand to clear it. The iron

Celebration

frame was too hot to hold on to anywhere for support. It would have blistered skin. I balanced awkwardly and pulled out handful after handful. From fingertips to shoulder the itch scalded my arm. I cried out in pain. One might have been robbing a beehive with bare arms.

One longed for night and a shower, then at the touch of water flinched away. Thousands of needles pierced at once.

When writing the Miss Strawberry verses for children I forgot to crutch our ewes before lambing. I kept down-to-earth enough to do the routine farming and moving of the irrigation sprays and see that the ewes were well. I would even have noticed, since big bellies and swelling udders are obvious, that they were about to lamb. But in welcoming Miss Strawberry I forgot the lambs would have difficulty pushing under woolly flanks to find teats on woolly udders, and that blood-stained woolly crutches attract blowflies.

Two of our children brought Miss Strawberry to live with us when they were four years old and six. They named her and told me stories about her. She took away their arms or legs and hid them. She would ask a friend to dinner and if he was not careful she would eat his toes. She quarrelled with people in her house, and even with parts of her house. Her old chimney was cranky, her path difficult. One walked along it towards the front gate and it slid off in the wrong direction. Her handbag was made of crocodile skin that she forgot to take the crocodile out of. Miss Strawberry was worth knowing.

One morning I did not take her with me round the sheep. I saw with full understanding a new-born lamb futilely circling its apparently featureless mother. All the lamb could find was a cylinder of wool on four short woolly legs. It was too late to drive them to the shed for crutching. A two or three day starve is bad for ewes in late pregnancy. The lambs already dropped might have been trampled on or separated from their mothers in yards and pens, so might any lambs born during crutching.

With the still-inexperienced lad who worked for me then I erected temporary yards near the ewes under a clump of Yellowbox trees on the river bank, spread a tarpaulin on the ground as a shearing board, loaded a portable crutching-plant on to the Land-Rover and backed it up to the tarpaulin. I had never done any consistent crutching, the lad had done a couple of short days only. We yarded the few ewes that had already lambed and as many others as we thought we could crutch in a day – about two hundred – and began. There was only one stand. I did ten, the lad did ten in turn.

A shearing handpiece buzzes at high speed. Hold it too tightly and it jars the hand, too loosely and it kicks free and swings about dangerously. Let it run out of the wool and it gets hot. It is driven by plastic cables, the long gut and the short gut, running inside jointed metal tubes. Pull it out at the wrong angle and the joints clatter and vibrate and the machine resists. Guide it back too sharply and the handpiece chatters and tries to twist away.

I would catch a ewe, sit her on her rump, pull her into position, take up the handpiece, jerk the rope that put it in gear, shear off any wool growing round her udder, take a light blow off each flank so the lamb could see under her, turn her so she sat on her left side, clean above her tail, across her crutch, down the right leg stiffened by my left fist thrust into her groin. The wool, tipped grey with dust and natural grease, is suddenly white as it rolls away from the handpiece. The comb should make a pattern of long straight lines in the short wool left next to the skin, and patches of pink skin should show how close the wool is shorn. The lines left by our inexpert blows were short and crooked and patches of blood showed here and there where the cutters had nicked the skin.

When the right leg was clean I would swing the ewe to face the other way and clean the left leg and the rest of her crutch. Unwilling sheep, cantankerous metal had to be moved in coordination. Maori shearers work so gracefully they make a ballet of the shearing. We sweated and worked hard. Our backs ached so much it was easier not to straighten till the tenth was done. While one straightened the other bent. But we crutched six hundred and felt satisfied, and the last one was crutched better than the first.

The river farm was our first farm, a soldier settler's block. It made the apparently wasted years in the army worthwhile. I had no money to buy a farm and four years' work at anything else would not have earned a farm. It was a joyful day inspecting it for the first time. We bogged in burr

Celebration

medic in a gully. It was our gully leading down to our stretch of river and it was our burr medic that our lambs would fatten on. Our giant River Red Gums grew by the river and water swirled over the roots of our own River Oaks. The boundary fences were lines of surveyors' pegs that the grass was growing over. There were no internal fences, no roads, no house, no water for the land off the river, no sheds, no yards. Where we built there would be no slugs in the gardens, no fleas waiting for the dogs, no ticks for the fowls. No one had ever lived on any part of it to nurture domestic curses. There was no money for building anything either. We had to make that before we could spend it. We did not grow crops, or sheep, or cattle: we grew a farm.

The memory of touch is as perfect as the memory of sight. I did not see the Brown Snake that struck at my face from a distance of fifteen centimetres. I heard a noise in long grass at the base of a water tank. It sounded like water spraying. I went down on my knees, parted the grass and scales slid along my right ear. The snake did not intend to kill me. It could not have missed my face. It struck to frighten me away and it struck so quickly sixty centimetres of scales scraped my ear before I rolled clear. I know forever the feel of an angry snake.

Riding in the rain – the horse is warm, the rain is cold – one is conscious of warmth radiating outwards from the inner thighs, of cold radiating in. Where is the dividing line? Will it to move outward. But it moves inward. The rain is colder than the horse is warm. The horse is getting cold, too. It humps its back as rain lashes its rump. If we were travelling the other way it would try to turn round to keep the rain out of its eyes. I am soaked. I cannot get wetter. But still I feel individual drops falling from my hair, on to my neck, sliding down my back. They make colder lines as far as my belt. My back feels striped with cold. Water runs into my boots. It tickles below the ankles, washes under the soles of my feet in rhythm with the horse. If I move, my buttocks squelch on the saddle. Hands begin to pucker. The reins feel mushy. I shorten them, squeeze my knees slightly. The horse breaks willingly into a canter. Mud flies from its

Touch and feelings

hooves into my hair, into my face, on to my legs. We settle back to walking. I try not to feel.

Yet sometimes I walk in the rain. I go out to see if water is flowing and where it is flowing. I go out to see the cattle drinking at new puddles instead of walking to the trough, and emus and kangaroos, too, welcoming fresh, close water. I watch mole crickets ridging the sandy soil as they tunnel just under the surface, and I watch which birds fly in the rain and which sit hunched on branches until it stops. I watch ants making late repairs to the mounds around their holes. Mostly I go out to feel the rain. One is part of the earth being rained on, and one is grateful.

If one has to work for hours in the rain a jute cornsack draped over the shoulders and fastened across the chest with a piece of tie-wire is the best cover of all. It keeps the shoulders dry, it leaves the hands free. Australian farmers have used them since farming began. Raincoats are heavy, one sweats inside them, after an hour or so all of them let in rain.

Grey flannel singlets have gone out of fashion. For about seventy years they were the badge of the Australian workman, drover, miner, timbergetter, shearer, stockman, labourer. 'No matter how cold and wet and miserable you are' a drover told me, 'a grey flannel singlet keeps you warm and dry and comfortable'.

An old stockman who once worked on the station our river farm was part of wore an oilskin raincoat on frosty mornings. He filled the pockets with hot, thick, mutton and barley stew. It warmed his thighs, warmed his hands in turn; and at lunch-time he scooped out handfuls and ate as he rode.

The word *feelings* is one of the wonders of the English language. It expresses what seems to be inexpressible. How can one explain an inner touch? One does not even know what is touched. It seems to be in the body, not in the head. Does a chemical move through the heart? It leaves memories as clear as a physical touch.

Bunum, a native-boy about twelve years old, did odd jobs in our camp at Gusap. Sometimes he stayed with us for several days at a time. He enjoyed the American cigarettes

Celebration

we gave him, he enjoyed the food. He carried batteries to the battery-charger and brought them back when they were charged. He baled out our slit trenches after heavy rain. He watched us, imitated us. He wanted to learn to read. He lived in a village only two hours walk away. Two or three times when he came for the day only, his old father came with him. He sat under a tree near the maintenance hut and chewed betel-nut. His face was lined. The creases at each corner of his mouth ran blood-red with juice. It blackened his teeth; made his tongue and the whole inside of his mouth crimson as one saw when he poked out his tongue for a ladle of lime.

Betel-nut, like alcohol, is a mild stimulant and eventually a narcotic. It is intensely astringent. A bite into the green fruit puckers the mouth. Often it is dried before it is chewed. Those who prefer it green use lime to neutralise it for that is what turns the colourless juice red.

The old man had had his lime bowl since he was a young man. It was a superb thing. He shaped a green gourd as it grew by binding it with strips of bamboo until it developed into a perfect long-necked flask. He pulled it while it was still green, cut off the stem, and hollowed out neck and bowl with sharpened bamboo canes. All the flesh had to be scraped from inside the vulnerable green shell. It was as fine a job as curetting a womb. Then it had to be oiled, smoked and rubbed as it dried.

He worked on it for weeks until it was amber-coloured and hard. Then he carved the bowl with linked symbols that connected him to his ancestors, and his future son and his son's son to him. It signified eternity. What I do now has been done and will be done. Then he oiled, smoked and polished it again till it had a gloss that would last several lifetimes. He set the neck with cowrie shells that he had to bargain hard for. At that distance from the sea they were particularly valuable. He had never seen the sea and the little shells might have begun their traded passage before his father was born. He finished the bowl by lining the mouth with long dogs' teeth. He shot about twenty-four dogs with bow and arrow to get sufficient matching teeth.

He carved the spatula out of limbom, the iron-hard thin black wood of a palm. He notched the under-surface so it would rattle over the teeth. As he sat and chewed and dreamt, he lifted the spatula occasionally and smiled as it rattled back into the bowl. It seemed to reassure him. It also signified his position in the village. Only important men were allowed to rattle their spatulas.

Bunum said his father had seen one of the signallers wearing a singlet. His father would like a singlet. How much would he have to pay for one? I had army singlets I never wore. The next time he came I offered him two for his lime bowl. He considered perhaps for ten minutes. He looked at the singlets, looked at the bowl. He rasped the spatula on the teeth. Then he quietly turned his palm down: no. So I threw in a pair of shorts that had lost most of their buttons and were fraying at the legs.

He handed me the bowl and walked away slowly, then he turned, said he had no more lime, and asked if I had bought the lime, too. I said no. How could he carry it? He laid a singlet flat on the ground, poured the lime on to it and bunched the singlet over the top of it with his fist.

I was not proud of the bargain. I had belittled him and his society. I had belittled myself since I had downgraded remarkable craftsmanship. With the advantage of thousands of years of civilisation I had traded at a barbaric level.

I caught a Yellow-footed Marsupial Mouse for an Australian Broadcasting Commission team to film. I had told the story of the great Pilliga forests in northern New South Wales in *A Million Wild Acres*. Now I had been asked to help make the forest live in film, a medium I knew nothing about. In good years these little mice are common in the forest though, since they are nocturnal, few people ever see them. They have yellowish legs and broad feet, and the older males are as tawny on the belly as an old possum. When they crouch the dark guard hairs stand out on their grey backs so that they look like little hedgehogs. They have very sharp, carnivorous teeth, light grey rings round the eyes, and they move fast with a bouncing gait.

The television film-makers came up after nearly two years of drought. I had fifty traps out baited with soaked dog biscuits or peanut-butter and bacon for ten nights to catch that one mouse. It was a beautiful specimen, a very big male, more tawny than usual. Phrases about him that I could use before the camera began to sing in my head: 'Look at him! He is an outstanding specimen, almost twice the usual size. He's one of those exceptional individuals animals depend on to carry the species through long droughts. Most of his kind are dead.'

I put him in a covered drum on the verandah and gave him layers of newspaper to shelter between. I fed him pieces of steak and all the meal-worms I could find. They also were in short supply. I turned over old bags and logs for a couple of hours each day. Other stories about him formed as I gathered his food. 'Nest winter he'll find a female survivor and mate with her. He's a savage lover. The females ovulate under shock. So he'll grab her between the shoulders with his teeth, drag her into position and mount. He'll ride her for up to twelve hours and if she tries to pull away he'll shake her about viciously, even tear strips of skin off her. He's got a strange split penis. The end forks into two prongs about eight millimetres long, one for each horn of the womb.'

When the television crew arrived a week later he was healthy and lively. We set up a fish-tank on the lawn with sand and twigs and leaves making a natural-looking background to film him against. I walled the sides in temporarily with cardboard boxes so he would not make a wild leap against the invisible glass and kill himself when he was released. We covered the top to shelter him from the sun. They seldom drink. They depend on the scant moisture in the insects they eat. So they keep to underground shelters by day where the atmosphere is more humid and come out to feed at night. They can retain their urine until it is extraordinarily concentrated.

The cameraman tested the light, focussed roughly. The sound engineer had fitted a tiny microphone inside my shirt and trailed wires to the transmitter in my hip pocket. We removed the boxes and the cover. The mouse ran about the cage. The cameraman made final adjustments, then cursed and called 'Cut!' The angle of the sun had changed and now the walls of the cage acted as mirrors. The lawn reflected in it, so did trees in the background. We covered the cage again, altered its position and masked the lawn with sheets of black polythene. We uncovered the cage again. The director

Touch and feelings

called 'Action!'. The assistant cameraman held up the clapboard with the take number on it. I began to tell what a fine mouse it was. The camera followed it as it bounced across the cage. Then it stopped in a corner, scratched at the sand, and dropped dead.

I had betrayed the wondrous tuning of its body to drought. It did not have the endurance of ten minutes of sunshine in reserve.

After the war ended on Bougainville our unit waited four months for those Liberator bombers to take us home. Two of us formed the 1 Aust. Mobile Bookmaking Company. We made a unit pennant and put it up outside our tent. We scorned to bet starting-price. The S.P. bookmakers in the islands had a hard time of it. Island favourites were often different to mainland favourites and the S.P. bookies had no control over prices. Bert, my partner, had been a bookmaker's penciller. We laid our own prices and we never refused a bet. We made good profits on the days the starting price bookmakers lost. But we had to be mobile to keep the book balanced. Bert would shout the name of a horse, hand me a roll of notes, and I would run for the nearest Jeep and drive round the other bookmakers laying off what it was not safe to hold.

But the army began to frown on 'unauthorised use of vehicles'. Wartime extravagance was over. The military authorities were saving up for the leaner times of peace. So I paid an American fifty dollars for a Jeep he was supposed to drive to a burial pit under laws made to ensure no civilians got any advantage out of unwanted and abandoned army equipment. I hid it in the jungle within reasonable sprint distance. It had no clutch but I did not need a clutch to change gears in a Jeep. The engine was dependable. The body was so rusty I expected it to disintegrate every time I drove it.

One day Bert handed me a roll of the old five-pound and ten-pound notes. 'There's three and a half thousand quid there at 4 to 1. Get rid of it for Christ's sake. You've got twenty minutes.' We had begun with a thousand pounds; we had made four thousand. That horse could ruin us. And the first bookmaker wanted none of it. The next took the five hundred. I had time to reach one more only. He belonged

Celebration

to a unit ten kilometres farther down the road. The race was to begin in seven minutes.

The Jeep bounced. The holes in the floor widened and narrowed. Rust fell out of holes I did not know were there. Chunks of flooring littered the road behind me. I approached the bookmaker with suitable calm as the horses lined up at the barrier. He was glad to take the money.

The horse did not win. We could have held it all. But we still made a profit on the race. On the Melbourne Cup, it must have been November 1945, we laid a perfect book. No matter which horse won we won. After discharge we agreed we would pool our deferred pay and bookmaking profits, Bert would apply for his licence, I would go back to the land and remain mostly a sleeping partner in the business but would help out sometimes at busy meetings. And after discharge I was not brave enough to do it. Once back on the farm under the authority of the weather it seemed an outlandish occupation. I never saw Bert again. A shoot of my life shrivelled.

At the Channon market out of Lismore where one is offered bowls of delicate wild raspberries with thick illegal cream alongside a stall of tasteless, greasy hamburgers of sliced, pressed, frozen, boned meat between white papier mâché rolls, where the exquisite jostles the kitsch, the capable the incompetent, we found Rick Wilder who spins raw silk and Rick Rose Ritter who weaves it. They had set up a display under an immense tropical tree. Beautiful blouses, frocks, coats hung from the branches. Girls were stripping off and trying them on in the open. All the clothes were designed for the young with low necks and ragged hemlines. I asked Rick Rose if she would weave a dress for Joan. Oh yes, she would. What elements did we want woven into it?

'What elements do you offer?'

'Sometimes' she said 'we think of water as we work. We sit naked by a creek, dabble our feet, and cloth flows from our fingers. Our clothes fit beautifully when we think of water.'

'Make it as you feel on the day.'

When the frock arrived a note from Rick Rose said they had woven in sunshine and happiness. We had a happy night the first time she wore it. We went to a dinner and play at the Rothbury Estate in the Hunter Valley. No one knew us there and strangers kept coming up in wonder and asking if they could feel the frock. Rick Rose had sewn rough wooden buttons on it that made it look too informal. We replaced them with superbly-made pottery buttons. The wooden buckle on the belt we replaced with silver. It did not disperse the happiness.

'Your wife has a lovely figure, hasn't she?' said a plump girl who was looking at the dress on display at a craft exhibition.

'Oh yes, she has!' I have not got a figure to delight her. My imagination acts for me.

I went to school for the first time during the last two months of 1934. The school was in Chapel Street, Marrickville, of brick and bitumen dusted over by factories, with a brilliant teacher named Redmond. He found learning as much fun as I did. I was eleven years old, sent to school after four years of the Blackfriars Correspondence School for conditioning to a classroom before beginning at Fort Street Boys' High School. That school was then competitive. The barrier of the Primary Final surrounded it but I had no doubt of getting over it. The correspondence school had put me so far ahead of Charles Redmond's class I ignored what the others were doing and worked ahead on my own. What I mostly had to learn was the language of my classmates. It was an abrupt entry to the society of children.

On the first morning mother sent me with a new Globite case, new black shoes, new socks, new short trousers, new shirt, new blue blazer and a new white Panama hat with a blue band. A thin, dark, dusty boy watched me approach. His shirt was torn, his shorts frayed, and the left pocket was broken. The white lining protruded. He stood in a depression where the bitumen had cracked away on one side of the gate. He stirred dust and pebbles with bare big toes. I walked through the gate. He looked at my hat. He looked at his feet. He bent back both big toes and flicked a couple of pebbles towards me. 'Christ!' he said. 'Was it your old man's?'

I had never heard a father referred to as an old man. Correspondence school students in those years began work when they were seven years old. I learnt to read quickly then read constantly. I read Blake and Coleridge, de Quincey, Conrad, Melville, but nothing modern. I had watched all our animals breeding. I knew all of the medical terms for sex but none of the slang. I had the theory. The rest of the pupils had crude practicality.

The boy at the gate knew all of 'The Good Ship Venus'. He would recite it at lunch-time.

> Twas on the good ship Venus –
> My Gawd! – you ought've seen us:
> The figurehead was a whore in bed,
> The ensign a rampant penis...
>
> The cabin-boy was a source of joy
> And such a lively nipper.
> He stuffed his arse with broken glass
> And circumcised the skipper...

There were many verses. It was a wonder to hear. I experienced a new world. One day he made mysterious movements with the tip of a little finger hooded by two fingers of his other hand. 'Have you ever seen a little thing that looks like this?' It was years before I realised that somewhere he must have watched closely while a woman with an exceptionally big clitoris worked up to an exceptionally vigorous orgasm. But I think he experienced it as entertainment only. He had to mock the world to cope with it.

Kerry Jane's wedding was laughter and excitement and deep joy, too. We did more than pay for it: we made it. 'We want to get married in a couple of months' she said 'and I'd love to have the reception at home.' A wedding reception seemed to need something more than the many visitors who come and fit in. I looked hard at the house.

I write unaware of my surroundings. I need a solid chair to sit on, a table that does not wobble, my books, my two fountain pens, a vital partner to meet me on earth when both our work is done. Apart from that I go wherever I am writing about. That is where I live. That is what I see. The house is no more than a shield from the discomforts that would hinder thinking.

Touch and feelings

'Do you live in an old house?' someone asked me over pre-dinner drinks in a fine old Melbourne home.

'Oh yes' I said.

'How old?' asked somebody else interestedly.

I realised what was meant and laughed. 'About 1923' I said. 'Our house is not old in the good sense of old. Dilapidated would best describe it.'

An amateur carpenter built it. Unpractised builders added to it several times. There is always somewhere cool to sit on the wide verandahs but they sag a bit now. The whole house sprawls lopsidedly. Several detached rooms are connected by a broad covered walkway with a cement floor. There is sufficient area where the roof does not leak for shelves to hold several thousand books. There are enough cool dark corners for good wines to age in their cardboard boxes with the year of the first permissible opening marked on the flaps in imperial figures by a thick felt pen. There is a big kitchen with big windows, a big slow-combustion stove and an electric stove, and three big refrigerators to store fresh food. The plumbing in the bathroom is crazy. One showers through a maze of brass taps. The pipes to the septic tank block with roots at the most inconvenient times.

And now the walkway roof was missing. Two or three years before it had collapsed one very wet night. The decaying pine slabs that covered it looked good but they had at last absorbed more weight of water than the trusses could bear. A creaking and splintering woke us all up, a crash and the sound of splashing water got us out of bed. The falling roof had broken a hot water pipe. In the morning I helped clear away the several trailer loads of broken timber. I sleeved and soldered the hot water pipe. I went back to my writing and forgot about it.

'Did you know the north wall of the kitchen has got no paint on it at all? We're back to bare boards.'

'It's been like that for years.'

'Has it?'

'And there's a board broken on the back verandah where a lot of people will be walking.'

'We've been dodging it for months.'

'Oh!'

Luckily both sons were home on vacation. There was a

Celebration

friend having a break from university who had been working for us all the year and an agricultural student from the University of Adelaide learning some practicality to go with her brilliance. We painted. We pulled down an unwanted houseyard fence, a job we had postponed often. A builder refloored the verandah while we lifted out the old uprights of the walkway with a tractor and a long chain. The posts supported a wire trellis overgrown with grapes coming into fruit, and an old wistaria that threatened to overgrow everything. We wanted it to look undisturbed. So we handled the heavy new five-metre ironbark posts as though they were as fragile as theatre props, stood them up without bumping the vines and rammed them solid. When the trellis was strained to them not a leaf seemed to be missing. The builder covered it with galvanised iron, so suitable for the Australian inland since it quickly loses its ugly shine and tones with the sky.

We wrote our own wedding invitations on handmade paper, folded rough-torn envelopes about them and sealed the flaps with wax. We drove two hundred and fifty kilometres to persuade an excellent caterer to travel that distance and do better than she had ever done. We planned school prawns and cold cucumber soup for the hot January night, well-fed porkers baked whole in a wood-fired baker's oven, farm chickens, wholemeal buns that her partner baked along with white French loaves, and imaginative salads, chopped pears steeped in real mayonnaise, zucchini and tomato, cucumber and white grapes, platters of little boiled new potatoes with chopped parsley stuck in a varnish of butter. She agreed, if we sent her the recipe and a bottle of the right port wine, to make Cumberland sauce to go with the pork, that thin, slightly sweet, sharp sauce of port wine, wine vinegar, cayenne pepper, orange and lemon juice, and a little of the thinly-sliced peel boiled together and reduced till it lost individual flavours. For pudding she would make a syllabub of white-fleshed clingstone peaches and farm cream curdled with French sauternes.

In Sydney our daughter found a dressmaker happily opening her shop after a long illness. She made a cream wedding gown with a difficult skirt of little pleats as though it was a joy, not a business. We all went to cellars where we are

Touch and feelings

well known and spent an afternoon looking at the food list and tasting and selecting wines to suit. We had real wine, an imaginary feast.

Then we went looking for material for the frocks of the bridesmaid and matrons of honour. They wanted to make their own. Too many bridesmaids look as though they have been iced, not dressed. A cream Chinese silk with a hazy, tawny pattern through it looked cool and different. Our purchase left little on the roll. The shopgirl put away a scrap of cloth that was to become important.

Home again we booked all the rooms at both the local hotels. Our town is too out-of-the-way to support a motel. We erected a seven-metre cement cattle trough to hold bottled beer and ice. We ordered one and a half tonnes of ice from the nearest ice-works. We borrowed four or five spare refrigerators from friends, awkward things to load and unload, and hard to rope steady on the Land-Rover on the rough gravel roads. The septic tank would not cope with over a hundred people so we dug a pit, fitted it with an old-fashioned seat, and walled it with hessian. Rent-a-loo had not then reached the country.

Two days before the wedding a tearful matron of honour rang from Moree. 'Do you think there was enough of that material left to make two sleeves? You know I always work in a bit of a muddle. Well last night I sewed till late and I went to bed leaving everything on the floor. Tim got up early and he tidied up. He picked up all the bits and pieces, and the sleeves I'd cut out had got mixed up with them. He burnt them.'

Kerry Jane behaved sensibly: she laughed. Then she rang the bridesmaid who lived in Sydney. 'I'm sure they'd have that scrap of material left. Would you go in and buy it, then bring it up a day early so we can have the sleeves cut out ready for Margie when she gets here?'

The morning of the wedding was a well-planned scramble. Someone drove seventy kilometres in one direction for the ice. Kerry and I drove seventy kilometres to an orchard in another direction for peaches. The boys erected hired tables and chairs in the garden and strung up extra lights. The matron of honour stitched her sleeves. Joan drove the other girls to decorate the little local church with

Celebration

bunches of oat grass in seed, that lovely native with heavy fawn heads borne on purple stems.

Then, unreally, it was time to get dressed, to tie my bow tie (a modern one with wide wings because one of my sons had borrowed my old slim tie), to sit with my daughter in the back of a driven car. At the church gate we grouped in the conventional order and approached the entrance to the church. The bridal veil threatened to fall off. We stopped in the vestibule to adjust it. Kathy, the bridesmaid, moved forward and peeked into the church. The short aisle grew into a long tunnel with the bridegroom and his groomsmen waiting at the far end. The little church broadened into a cathedral. 'Oh my Gawd!' said Kathy. 'I could never get through getting married.' Kerry laughed. Everyone in the church heard.

That set the tone for the whole wedding. The day itself was as good as the preparation. There were no speeches, no formal photographs, just talk, laughter, extended eating and drinking, and serious moments, too. What else is a wedding but an accentuation of life? At about one o'clock in the morning I began to make pot after pot of real coffee. At two o'clock the caterers left, happy as the wedding guests. By three o'clock most had gone home or to the hotel rooms in town. Twenty or so stayed, sleeping in what beds there were, on mattresses on the verandah, in the backs of station wagons. Some still sat and talked.

We went to bed. Joan heard a noise in the kitchen. She dozed, heard it again, slept soundly for an hour or so. She got up at daylight. The jaws of pigs, their backbones, breastbones of chickens, cucumber peel, filter bags spilling coffee grounds, aluminium foil, greaseproof paper, a broken plate, prawn shells, stones of olives, empty bottles, slices of pork fat, scraps of bread – the grotesque skeleton of the feast was scattered all over the kitchen floor. Pepper, the Beagle bitch that grew up with our daughter, had scented her way through an open door and emptied the two garbage bags I had not bothered to move. She had eaten till her belly nearly sagged to the floor, waddled into the next room, and there she slept.

Now that our three children are married, or about to be married, to white Australians, I wondered what my reaction

Touch and feelings

would have been if they had wanted to marry an Asian or Aboriginal or one of the stern-mannered European races. I found my attitude illogical. It would not have concerned me if my sons had wanted to marry a girl of any race, yet I would have been concerned if our daughter had wanted to marry a foreign man. Since I am about to begin writing a human history of the Chinese in Australia and the difficulties of last century's mixed marriages come into it, I need to account for my feelings. I think it is because women are less self-important than men. Their culture influences their disposition not their dignity. So they are more adaptable. A change in ways affects them but does not affront them.

After her marriage our daughter got her pilot's licence. She flew us north-east over the Nandewar Ranges to Murwillumbah on the North Coast of New South Wales. Commercial flights do not go that way. For the first time I looked down on mountains I had looked up to since I was a boy. One long hill we had known as the naked woman – long hair thrown back, forehead, eyes, nose, lips, chin, neck, breasts, belly with sunken navel, pubic hair, thighs, knees, legs, feet – became not one hill but a succession of hills that I should have understood from contour maps. Castle Top, or Mount Courada, a huge stone cube on top of a dome, was even more impressive from above than from below, and Mount Kaputar, the highest peak, was insignificant, one of several little humps. It was not definite which hump. We saw where creeks began and where they became rivers. For one hour we watched jagged hills where there was nowhere to land if an engine failed, nowhere to glide to. On the coast, since she did not have an instrument rating, she flew round heavy, floating clouds that can disorient a pilot flying visually in seconds, or else flew under them, then made an exploratory pass over the difficult strip at Murwillumbah. As she circled to land, the strip disappeared among buildings. She lined up from memory, and when the strip appeared again, she dropped over tall trees bordering a creek, over a row of buildings, a fence, then down on to a short strip reluctantly bare of the sugar cane that walls it in.

I wanted to learn to fly when I was in the army and thought once of transferring to the air force. When our Armoured Divison was stationed near the old Lowood aerodrome out

Celebration

of Ipswich in Queensland, I went up with RAAF pilots practising dive-bombing whenever I was off duty. They flew Wirraways, that slow, clumsy, Australian-built two-seater praised by the politicians of the day as a marvel of Australian engineering. Already they were as out-of-date as our discarded light horses. But in the bombing dive from five thousand feet to three thousand I rode a plunging falcon and the plane screamed as we pulled out. My weight flowed into my boots till I feared they would drop through the cockpit floor and heavy, dead hands pressed my knees. Always before I had recovered, the pilot was hanging his head out the side of the plane to see where the bomb had dropped. And always, when turning with sharply-tilted wings or coming in to land, I felt so giddy I could not have handled the controls. So I decided I would make a hopeless pilot.

It is good watching one's children develop talents one has not got. The thing most worth teaching them consciously seemed to be the more one learnt the better one experienced life. And unconsciously one passes on more than a half share of oneself. Kim as a veterinarian is a fine surgeon, capable of quick, delicate work my hands were not made for. Mitchell directs aircraft in calculated patterns that amount to playing quick-move chess with planes in flight and dives under the sea for relaxation in complicated interludes that are a delight to the meticulous and disaster to the careless. Joan is remembered with delight in pharmacies hundreds of kilometres apart. We meet with disparate skills and we interest each other.

Before the gross, omnivorous European Carp spread through the western rivers of New South Wales, we fished with light lines for the four good-eating Australian fish, Murray Cod, Fresh-water Catfish, Golden Perch or Yellowbelly, and Silver Perch. The state of the water, the bait, the touch on the line told us what fish was biting before we caught it. In summer when the Namoi River was low and clear on our own farm, Yellowbelly bit in deep shaded holes by day, on the edge of the slow current by night. They took yabbies that we swept out of farm ground tanks with a prawn net, or the big, hard blacksoil worms we dug in the crumbly soil under spherical bushes of dead, blow-away roly-poly. The worms were up to forty centimetres long and twelve millimetres in diameter. We threaded half worms on the hooks so that the undamaged end wriggled clear of the point to attract the cautious Yellowbelly.

After a twenty-minute wait one would feel a slight scraping on the line. A Yellowbelly was circling, watching the bait. Then there would be a pulsing of the line as the fish held itself steady over the worm and fanned it with its fins. Sometimes it then swallowed the bait and swam hard for the nearest snag as soon as it realised a line was attached. Usually it played with the fisherman for another hour or so. It would fan for five minutes, nibble at the bait, pick it up lightly in its mouth, put it down, fan it, nibble it, pull it a few centimetres, put it down, nibble it, fan it, pick it up and run with it for three metres, put it down. One could see the fish through line and fingers. One had to be patient. Jerk the line and the Yellowbelly might swim away offended. When it was ready it swallowed bait, hook, sinker and several centimetres of line, then ran.

One pulled it out quickly lest it wrap the line round a snag, cut the line off at the mouth since fish are better kept alive till one is ready to clean them, dropped it into a light jute bag, put the bag in the water and pegged its mouth firmly in the mud at the water's edge.

Then one threaded on another sinker, tied on another hook, rebaited and waited for the next fish to begin its long game. When the Barwon River is rising in flood, and the usually milky water is deep grey, brown or cream according to which tributary river has flooded it, Yellowbelly feed voraciously in the quieter water near the steep, bare, white, clay banks. Then they swallow the bait without hesitation and one can take six or seven good fish in an hour.

Whenever I think of fishing, especially if it has been several months between trips, I can feel line in the hand: the gladdening tug of nylon over the right forefinger if one is handlining; if one is fishing with a rod, the slipping between thumb and forefinger of the left hand of two or three metres of lightly held line stripped off the reel so a nervous fish gains confidence.

We fished for Murray Cod in winter after the first heavy frost somehow made them interested in our baits and we

Celebration

fished with live Common Carp of a size no other fish would swallow. Some nights I would sit for four or five hours and feel nothing more than the constant futile wriggling of the little fish on the hook, and when my hands got too cold to feel even that, I would go home to bed. Sometimes after an hour or two one would feel a flurry of the bait fish, then a gentle, slow drawing-out of the line. One was conscious of power. More than the little carp was pulling. The line might move fifteen metres upstream or ten metres down. Often that was the end of it. The cod was not hungry. But occasionally the speed of the run increased and one began to feel weight on the line. Then one lifted the rod. It bent. The line sang; the ratchet slipped. One brought it in slowly but as firmly as the line allowed. It was essential to keep the cod's head facing the bank, not its favourite logs. Once in shallow water, if given a chance, a cod lunges forward, rolls, twists, turns round, lashes its tail, snaps the line, and is free. So one picks up the gaff as it nears the bank, keeps the rod bent hard, takes up line, and as silver breaks the surface, one swings the rod round with the left hand to keep the line taut while the right hand strikes hard with the cruel gaff. Out comes four kilogrammes, ten kilogrammes, of beautiful spotted fish. Little brown marks pattern each side. There is a pleasant legend that each cod wears a map of its place in the river.

On our river farm I knew which log each of our giant uncatchable cod lived under. Riding along the river bank one sometimes saw them swimming home after a cruise on the surface. One afternoon when fish were biting I cast a big silver lure beside a log where I knew a six-kilogramme cod lived. It was an unknown fish that came up. The water boiled. Something thudded against the spoon, tossed it two metres out of the water, then a tail forty centimetres wide broke the surface as a huge cod dived back under the log.

One cod that weighed about forty kilogrammes played with me for most of one night. I had been fishing with rod and light line for catfish on a big, shallow, silty platform where a creek joined our river. Catfish make one or two quick, experimental tugs at the bait, then swallow it. Once hooked they charged about in the shallow water, even leaped out of it at times. By nine o'clock I had caught as many as

Touch and feelings

I could carry the couple of kilometres back to where I had left the Land-Rover. Driving home beside the river I noticed that the half moon threw the spear-shaped shadow of a River Oak from the bank to a log where a cod lived. I could sit in that shadow where it could not see me. Perhaps that night when fish were biting so well, an uncatchable cod might be caught. In a stock trough near the house I had a red Common Carp about thirty-five centimetres long, big enough to interest such a fish. I drove home for a heavy handline and the carp.

I stuck a stout, springy green stick into the muddy bank in the depth of the shadow, tied the line to it so that it was a couple of metres shorter than the distance to the cod's log, hooked on the bait fish with one big hook in the back, another in the tail, and threw it in with a splash near the bank. Within a minute the cod picked it up, ran with it towards the log, jerked the line as it tightened so that the top of the springer bent into the water, jerked it again even harder, then put the bait down. I pulled the line in towards the bank. The cod picked up the bait again. I held the line. The cod jerked it out of my hand. I held it with both hands. The cod pulled so hard and so suddenly I lost balance and clutched at roots to save me going into the river.

The cod held the live carp so that the hooks were clear of its mouth. If it had been able to tear it free, it would have swallowed it. For seven hours it played with the bait. It sucked at it, butted it, fanned it, swam after it, jerked it, ignored it for twenty minutes, came back. The shadow of the tree was behind me, running up over the bank, and the shadow of the opposite bank was approaching the centre of the river, when seven ducks landed in the water above the cod. There was a swirl underneath them. Six ducks flew away, one disappeared. The cod had fed. The game was over. I released the carp that was still very active. It had earned its freedom.

Once we went by night into the Warrumbungle mountains and fished a mountain creek for the sweet, scaleless, slimy River Blackfish we had never tasted. They are plentiful there but they are becoming rare in most New South Wales streams. They are much smaller than the bait we use for Murray Cod and they bite so gently one sometimes does not realise

Celebration

they are on the line. We caught up to a dozen in shallow rocky pools no bigger than a bath tub. Slim and about twenty centimetres long, they croaked like frogs as we lifted them on to the bank. It is cool in the mountains on the dark summer nights when they bite best. It was good testing pool after pool. When we lost the tiny streams that connected one pool to the next, we did not switch on a torch and frighten the fish, we zigzagged about feeling for water or listening for the whisper of its flow. The fish bit in the narrow shallows as well as in the pools. It was like fishing in a dish. One threw the baited hook towards where one thought the water was, then felt along the line to make sure it was in the water.

European Carp have spoilt our touch. We still fish the western rivers but now we use much heavier line and we no longer always know what is biting. A fifteen-kilogramme carp will take a remnant of worm one centimetre long or a big black yabby twenty-two centimetres long. We can no longer cast light lines baited with small wriggling worms on small hooks into running water to take the active Silver Perch. A big carp is more likely to take the bait and break the line or cut one's forefinger to the bone as one takes the line in hand to bring the fish to the bank. They look unpleasant with coarse scales and concertina lips. They taste worse. And they have vicious bones scattered through them shaped like the long-spined burrs of Cathead.

The piles of papers that I sort on our double bed when I am writing I transfer to the floor. They are labelled with chapter and subject. I arrange them in the writing room to give me access to my table and chair. The low piles I space so I can step over them conveniently, the high piles I put out of my path. As I need a pile I lift it on to the table, reread it, resort it, put the immediate papers on my left-hand side, notes about them on my right-hand side, the papers I need next in front of me, the rest in order about my chair. I work with copies of original documents, occasionally with the original document, with letters original and copied, books, pamphlets, leaflets – a mass of stuff that I will not transfer to a characterless card index. My imagination, my understanding works best among a jungle of papers.

As each pile is dealt with I pack them away in cardboard

boxes with their labels. A low pile might have stood in my path for six months. Now it is gone. I miss it. A high pile stood in one corner for two years. Now it is gone. The room looks gap-toothed.

From the time I begin to plan a book, phrases sing in my head. I write most of them down at once, stopping the car, the tractor, getting out of bed. I write chapter and subject reference over them in red ink, and put the slip of paper in a big, brown envelope. After several years of research envelopes are crammed with torn-off strips of paper. The phrases I like best I do not write down. I say them to myself over and over. I say them as I go to sleep, I say them when I wake at night, I say them in the morning. I know where the phrase is to fit in the book. I will sing it over and over for three or four years of research, then, some time, I will put it down in its place.

And when it is written down I miss it. It looks marvellous on paper. The words before it and after it glow because of that one good sentence. One writes up to it and lets down gradually after it. It has to be given a setting. But in my head there is a gap. The sentence has been pulled out. I feel the space. My head is uncomfortable. Then wondrously another phrase begins to sing, and another. Spaces fill in, rearrange themselves. One is conscious of heightened thinking, heightened feeling. Words come with delight. Yet one must welcome them cautiously, deal with them moderately, or else they will cavort of their own accord. One can sit for two hours living words with all one's senses, seeing sentences, paragraphs, pages turning, a miracle of illusive print, till suddenly all one sees is the blank page beneath one's hand, and all one feels is an impression. The words that built it have evanesced. So the slow hand has to control the excitement in the head, force it to the production of solid images.

Sigmund Freud's search for power in cocaine, Aldous Huxley's experiments with mescalin bewilder me. What Huxley describes I feel naturally when I am writing. I live far above myself.

Writing exhausts one. It rarely disappoints one. When I had written twenty thousand words of *They All Ran Wild* I sent them to Douglas Stewart to see how the book was going. The next sentence was in my head. The papers were stacked.

Celebration

Pad lay open on the desk, my pen ready on top of a numbered page. The typescript came back the same week with no covering letter. I searched through the wrapping paper for a mislaid note – nothing. I thought it had been rejected. For two days I felt truncated. I had nothing to think about, nothing to do with my hands. My feet moved on spongy ground. Then disbelief took over. I rang Angus and Robertson. John Abernethy, the imaginative editor who died so young, answered the telephone.

'Didn't you like it, John?'

'Yes, of course we liked it. Get on with it!'

'The manuscript came back without any note.'

'The packagers are faster than the typists. A letter's on the way.'

So the world was remoulded. But it is always a cold wait for the first reaction to the first words of a new book. The last book makes the next book vulnerable.

In the confusion of feeling leading up to work on *They All Ran Wild,* among the jumble of advice, I came on the cryptic words of Havelock Ellis: 'The devil most often appears to a man in the guise of his wife and children.' I quoted them somewhere. I think Havelock Ellis meant that too many men and women use the needs of their families as excuse for neglecting their talents. That is how I used the sentence. Joan misunderstood. 'I'm a devil' she said wildly. 'Do you still want me?'

'I don't want you without my books. You wouldn't want me, either. You'd see me gutless.'

I drove to Coonabarabran airport one Sunday morning to meet Nelson's promotions officer. We were to spend a week driving through north-west New South Wales selling *A Million Wild Acres* to shops from the back of a utility. Books no longer sell themselves. Authors have to risk themselves in the market-place. So I stacked six years of my life into the utility, a tender load.

I liked the look of the tall woman who got off the plane. She carried her sense of humour with her. I had never met her. She knew me only from books and photographs. The publisher's conventional accountants thought the exercise silly. Veronica's reputation for successful promotion was at stake. My dignity was at stake – what little my sense of the ridiculous allows me. As well as newspaper interviews, she had arranged television and live radio interviews. I do not naturally answer questions quickly. I spend time looking for the best words, the most interesting answer. I talk much as I write. For a whole week I had to be instantaneously interesting. There were going to be more than enough opportunities to make a fool of myself and of her.

Accustomed to the rigours of city media, Veronica was uneasy because we had no schedule. We had not even decided which town to go to first. I thought it seemed better to let things happen. Anyway, I do not work easily to schedule. Keeping the next appointment might well exclude something more interesting.

'We'll go for a drive in the forest this afternoon,' I told her. 'I'll show you as much as I can of what we'll be talking about. Tomorrow we'll have to fit bookselling in with drafting off cattle for sale. They are fat and they have to go to market. Tuesday morning we'll watch them sold if you would like to see a stock sale. Then we'll sell books and sell ourselves as hard as we can.'

So we drove into the forest and seemingly out of civilisation. It presents that part of Australia, not as it was before European settlement, but as a concentration of what it was. Life accelerated there and excluded alien things. We drafted the cattle, a simple job if those in the yard work quietly and confidently and keep in position, a difficult job if a rough voice unsettles the cattle, or a man moves out of place. A man only thirty centimetres out of position can turn a beast back into the mob at a gallop instead of walking it quietly through an open gate. Veronica sat on a top rail in jeans and watched intently. She changed into a promotions officer outfit and we sold autographed books successfully in the two nearest towns.

Then she rang the newsagent in a town seventy kilometres to the west. Had he got her advertising pamphlets? Would he like us to bring him in some autographed books? Newsagents are not usually happy men. He was sourer than most. He was too busy to bother reading anything publishers sent

Celebration

him. And no, he did not want any books. It was stupid trying to sell a book for twenty-five dollars in a country town.

Joan rang the pharmacist she sometimes worked for. 'Henry, would you sell some books for us?' 'How much profit do I make?' Veronica and I handed him ten signed copies half an hour before his shop closed. We went to a hotel for a celebratory brandy. We drove home. The phone rang. 'Send me in another twenty books. I sold four in the shop in twenty minutes, the rest at the pub on the way home.' Altogether he sold about one hundred and fifty. The selling of books is no longer the staid occupation it was.

So we all enjoyed our dinner. Veronica knew food, she knew wine. She knew her job but did not take herself seriously. It was clear we were going to have a good week. We left home with the load of books early the next morning and watched our cattle sold for a satisfying price. From vantage points behind the auctioneer we peered through rails to watch the unnecessarily secret gestures of the bidding fat stock buyers. It is an atmosphere that entranced me as a child and entrances me still, especially since it will soon be lost to the heartless reckoning of a computer. It was fun involving someone else.

Then we had lunch with a good friend, then we sold books. We would drive to a town, talk to a reporter in the newspaper office who was usually more expert at interviewing than one would expect. 'Now we'll just do this radio interview' Veronica would say, 'then we'll have a cup of tea.' We let down on the drive to the station, keyed ourselves up at the door. Veronica would sit lonely on an office chair beside a speaker in the vestibule, willing I did not let her down. I would go into the studio where an astonishingly busy announcer was at work. Country announcers have no assistant to pass them things, no technicians to change channels to bring in other broadcasts. One announcer had two sets of earphones on his head, two speakers beside him. He was fitting in the station's morning programme with the racing acceptances from Sydney and Brisbane. His chair ran on tracks. A push of his feet sped him between a cassette bank of advertisements and a stack of gramophone records, another push sped him back to his controls. He switched switches, he moved his chair backwards and forwards, then he took off his earphones and asked me questions. And with only two or three breaks for advertisements or lists of scratched horses we talked sensibly for half an hour.

I could tell from Veronica's face how well I had done. She usually looked pleased enough. At least we sold books. And in Tamworth we did not have to offer ourselves humbly to the television station. The television station looked for us. We drove out to a dusty road and put on an act for them.

'This is fun,' I said over one cup of tea. 'But it is ridiculous, isn't it?'

'Oh yes!' said Veronica. 'Never take it seriously. But most do. Not many have the right sense of proportion.'

In the late afternoon we had a brandy. We talked quietly. We healed the day's nervous scars. Then we went to the best restaurant in town, or the only restaurant, or to friends for the night. Next morning we drove on to a similar circuit somewhere else. We talked all the way or we sat silent all the way. There was no need to entertain one another. We left the bitumen road and took what might have been a blacksoil short-cut across north-west plains, and we ran into a maze of unmapped tracks on big grazing runs newly split up for farming. Gravel roads led nowhere but to the corners of paddocks with lines of tractors and tillage machinery parked until rain set them to work again. But we got to the next town in time to sell books. The cheques built up satisfyingly, more than enough to confound the sceptical accountants.

We had a drink at a sawmilling town in the heart of the forest and sat on high stools at the bar among sleeper cutters and mill hands. We drove back through narrow forest tracks at night. Kangaroos jumped dangerously out of the shadows beside us. Emus ran ahead of us till they were exhausted, stupidly afraid to run into the protection of the forest because the undergrowth slowed them down. A Spiny Anteater crossed the road, surprisingly tall and fast on the run. One usually sees them rolled into spiky, defensive balls. When we got out to watch it more closely, it stopped, hunched itself, raked at the ground under it, and almost disappeared from sight in a few minutes. A collar of sand rose round

Celebration

it as it sank. We drove home to the good food Joan could produce without apparent effort after a day at work. I opened special wines. We had all earned them.

The trip was a remarkable experience. We enjoyed ourselves. We did what we set out to do, and we did all we could do. Each put the other at risk and we trusted one another's abilities. I had never worked so intensely with anyone before. I live so intensely with Joan I scarcely know which is she and which is I. But our work is separate. She knows little more of my writing than I know of her pharmacy.

I would not enjoy working so intensely with a man; I would not enjoy it with many women. I run my own risks and I calculate them. It is strange exposing oneself because someone else expects it. One thing startled me. It was marvellous working at such a pitch for one week with a woman I thought so much of. Three weeks would be difficult, four weeks impossible. Tea in the morning would lose its salve, brandy in late afternoon its absolution. Tension would build round us in static charges. Sex only would release it; and the release would hurt too much.

We talked about this book on the trip. It was a book I was going to write some day. I had been making notes for it for two years. Phrases were singing. But where did the book begin, where end, how did things connect? Perhaps it would never be written. It was a book that ought to be written. Why had no one written it before – such a simple idea? Because it was impossible to write it. 'I don't see how it could be written' said Veronica, standing my doubts concrete before me. 'It would have no form.' I had to answer her. 'It doesn't have to have any form. One cannot order the senses.' And the book came together.

Australian houses impose on the landscape. Suburban houses line up along the streets, lawns shaven, windows washed, roofs trim, doors closed, as though mustered by drill sergeants. 'Squad, atten-shun! From the right, number!' How many councillors would approve a house built back-to-front? They would fear it might fart at them.

Country houses are collections of coloured boxes dropped in paddocks. They could never have grown out of the soil. Dwellers in them are not so much protected as parcelled up.

Touch and feelings

I would like to build a house of big blocks of our own light salmon-pink soil. Door and window architraves would be unplaned, deep-red ironbark cut as solid as railway sleepers. There would be clear glass and stained glass in the windows. Superb modern craftsmen are at work with glass. One side of the house would be covered with horizontal ironbark boards to set off the pink earth with a deeper tone, and elsewhere upright slabs of yellow-brown cypress pine would break the line across a room or two. The floor would be of hard, narrow, dark brigalow parquet opening on to wide, polished cypress pine boards with brown knots swirling in a yellow glow. The roof would be of galvanised iron to match the sky.

We will probably never build the house. Building books in Australian is seldom profitable enough to build houses. Would it make life gladder? I do not see how it could.

Smell

By mid-October 1969 there was the alkaline smell of wheat ripening in the paddocks. Wheat ripens from the ground up. The lowest leaves yellow at the tips. Over three weeks or so the colour spreads. The leaves curl, droop. Colour runs up the stalks instead of sap, through the heads out into the awn. The swollen grain turns yellow-green. The leaves go papery. The grain gives up moisture, shrinks, deepens in colour to golden brown. The yellow stalks can no longer hold the heads upright. Crimps form where the stalk narrows below the head and the heads fold over and hang towards the ground. Four or five days later the grain is hard and ripe, the paddocks golden.

On 14 October 1969 the wheat had been colouring for nearly a fortnight. The skin of the grains was hardening, the sloppy white dough inside was getting stiffer each day. The crops were heavy. The air was summery. There had been no cold weather for six weeks. A rich harvest was only three weeks away. On the night of 15 October the heaviest frost known in north-west New South Wales froze the soft centres of the grains. As they turned to ice they swelled and burst the seed casings. Taps froze inside the house. Water in the stock troughs froze solid. A little water-cooled tractor, seemingly safe inside a shed, cracked its engine-block as the coolant froze. This is a common mishap. No one knew wheat could be damaged once the grains were turning.

By eleven o'clock the next morning the sun had melted the ice. The paddocks smelt unfamiliar and wrong. Each grain oozed its contents. None were whole. Two days later it rained. The damaged grain fermented. The farm stank of sour dough; or was it of dead hopes?

Before the 1955 flood drowned our river farm, the burr medic was sixty centimetres high and so dense it was difficult to walk through. Sheep balked at it. It tangled their legs. We had been moving the cattle into paddocks first to shorten

Smell

the feed for the sheep. It was a rich year. It smelt rich: damp earth and lush growth.

When I came back into the house after the flood, five centimetres of mud lay on the floor. Little fish were set into it like fossils. The house smelt mouldy.

As the water receded from the paddocks, two or three long lines of litter marked the heights the water held at for a few hours. It fell in stages. There were wracks of logs, wooden fence posts, cans of all sizes, 44-gallon drums, sawn timber, saucepans, doors, chairs, bottles full and empty, everything one might have found somewhere on farm or in town house. Also in the line, now so much rubbish, were dead sheep, dead cattle, pigs, hares, fowls, a turkey, a snake, a guinea-pig, fish, turtles, shrimps, yabbies. A drowned cow smells different to a drowned ewe or a drowned pig or snake. Each smells different to the same animal that has died differently. Collectively they stank of warm, soggy, putrid flesh.

The burr medic did not die and dry out. As the water left it, it collapsed into a brown slime and smelt more bilious than any animal. The paddocks might have been monstrous stinkhorns capped with an evil coating.

There was no telephone and no electricity to power pumps to help with the cleaning up. After a week when I had moved some of the mud out of the house and burnt the nearest of the dead animals with the nearest driftwood, when the slimy paddocks had begun to dry and the smell was sullenly unpleasant instead of fearsome, Joan came home with our new-born son. Until the torn-down power line was rebuilt, she cooked on a kerosene primus; we lit lamps at night. The smell of kerosene joined the smell of flood. It seeped into the walls of the house. For years afterwards humid weather brought the smell out again. Our noses relived the flood.

It is good to eat in big country kitchens. Guests can talk and drink and smell the food cooking. A lifted lid releases excitement and expectancy. No matter how often one smells them, onion and garlic turning golden in oil smell good. One tests the air to see what meat will be browned with them. The kitchen influences the house. It draws one with

Celebration

webs of odours. One walks towards it down corridors of smells.

In a corner of our kitchen end-of-season herbs hang drying in paper bags to fill in the gaps in the fresh herb supply. Each bag suggests a food. Smell them. Snf? Bay leaves – chicken in white sauce. Snf? Dill – cold cucumber soup. Snf? Basil – baked fish. Snf? Thyme – rabbit in white wine. Game can cope with thyme. Snf? Tarragon – sauce tartare. Rosemary is a perennial. There is no need to dry it. Pluck a shoot as one walks past it. Crush it. One smells a leg of lamb baking. Before we were married I drove her in one night to catch a train back to the city. Driving home alone I smelt rosemary in the car. She had bruised a sprig and stuck it behind the rear vision mirror so I would not forget her. There was no fear of that.

Farm kitchens smell of mushrooms periodically. Their odour acknowledges the soil. One would think the ground itself had fruited. After several days of rain and warm weather, a few hours at 16°C brings them up in clusters, in lines, scattered, in half arcs, quarter arcs, in big perfect fairy rings showing how the mycelium spreads underground. We go out with plastic buckets, lift them between index finger and second finger, pinch off the muddy ends of the stems and pull out any spiky seeds of khaki weed or clinging cylindrical pods of medic. One can fill a 9-litre bucket in an hour. Hands go brown with spawn. They smell brown. Mushrooms add dimension to a drab colour.

If one cooks meat or cabbage during the daytime in summer, big brown blowflies come to the kitchen windows, to the gauze on the closest verandahs. Urgent with maggots, they thump droning against the barriers. They crawl across the windows, testing the corners for a way in. What if a window cracked, the gauze yielded? It is more pleasant to cook at night. There is activity against gauze and window-panes then, too. Moths, grasshoppers, beetles, a mass of different insects swarm at the barriers. They come to light, not to smell.

Going to milk on a summer morning, a swarm of little black bushflies accompanies one. They settle on one's back, hoping for sweat to yield some of the animal protein they need to breed. They probe at the corners of the mouth, of

Smell

eyes. Wave them away. They circle the hand, come back. One cannot wave quickly enough to keep them away. It is better to ignore them. Fly, you are not tickling my lips. Fly, two flies, three flies – Good God! How many flies? – I know you are drinking at my eyes. I will not even blink. Swallow one and it cannot be ignored. Mouth, throat, stomach over-react. Admittedly a fly's legs multiply as soon as it gets in the mouth. A swallowed fly has more legs than a centipede. But it is a small thing. One does react absurdly.

In the yard some of the flies on one's back join the swarm about the cow. She promises more protein. Australia's bushflies welcomed the smell of the first European animals. They bred in their manure and increased in numbers to welcome them sufficiently. They line up along the backbone of the cow in the bail. Her lips are lumpy, eye-lids warty with flies. They drink the milk as it rises in the bucket. Now and again a jet hits one, buries it in froth. When the bucket is full, the froth is spotted black. The flies strain out.

In winter the flies are gone. Most die. Northern Australia replenishes the south at the beginning of spring. The air smells cold on a frosty morning. One welcomes the smell of cow. She smells warm. The milk smells of cow. It is a comforting smell. It eases the pain of cold hands. Many a black dairymaid on inland stations sat on the milking-stool, put her cold bare feet in the empty bucket, and milked quickly. When the milk reached her shins, her feet were warm.

The cow proves her calf by smell when it gallops out of the pen to drink the one teat left for it. She knows it by sight, she recognises its call. Smell is the final assurance, the most certain test.

A bull tries his cows by smell. As a cow lifts her tail to urinate, he trots across to her, sniffs at the stream, rejects her. He smells the vulvas of a couple of others as he moves past them, tests the urine of another, pokes his tongue out, tastes it, rolls his lips back, sniffs again. Then he licks her, moves round in front of her, licks her face with long strokes, chins her shoulder, moves behind her again, licks her, tries to mount. She excites him long before he excites her. She moves off to graze, walking quickly and snatching mouthfuls at intervals. He has to hurry to keep up with her. Whenever

Celebration

she stops he tries to mount. She moves from under him. His penis prods air, spatters lubricating fluid. He drops to ground and follows her again. She might keep him busy for two hours before she stands. Then after three or four quick mounts, when he stands resting, belly heaving, she backs into him, impatiently demanding more.

Wherever an animal moves it leaves traces of itself behind, gases, moisture, invisible flakes of skin. A snake smells keenly but it appears to taste its way about. It pokes out its forked tongue. Whatever is in the air collects on it. The snake pulls it back, lifts it and sinks the tips into two sensitive pits in the roof of the mouth. They record what the tongue has collected. A snake has no taste buds. The pits accentuate the sense of smell. When a snake is hungry the tongue flicks continually, testing. If a mouse has crossed a path two hours before, the snake's tongue collects the image, and the snake turns and follows it.

In Papua New Guinea earth tremors ran up the Markham valley and down the Ramu. The flat-floored valley was mostly treeless and about ten kilometres wide. Mountains bordered the north side. The south side was bordered by a strip of jungle, the wide sunken bed of the Ramu, more jungle, then mountains. The valley was a sea of green Kunai grass about two metres tall.

First there was silence. One heard the world go still. Many minutes later, looking out, one could see a rolling line in the distance, a tidal wave of grass. Did it bear loose grass with it? Would one be rolled under a breaker of grass? The jungle broke apart in long gashes, then lashed together again. Trees shivered ahead of the wave and behind it. Birds screamed. The ground trembled. Buildings rocked. As the wave rolled underneath one had to hold out one's hands to balance. Then came the smell of sulphur. Where did it come from? Did the wave carry the smell with it or did the disturbed earth puff gases out of its hot centre? The world looked stable again. The wave had receded out of sight. But the smell troubled us. We felt fragile.

We walked down a track in the Warrumbungle mountains in north-west New South Wales into a narrow valley with a little creek at the bottom. The air was humid, heavy and

Smell

unmoving. Five billy-goats grazed together on the hillside about a hundred metres off the track. Shaggy and big-horned, white, black, and patterned brown, they were fine-looking animals. But they were stripping shrubs that emus and wallabies eat gently and harmlessly. The goats bashed fruit down with their horns, stood on hindlegs to bare the leaves on top branches or trampled springy branches down with their forelegs and stood on them while they browsed. Goats are inordinately destructive and are out of place in wild Australia.

Two-thirds of the way down the track we ran into the smell of the goats. It seemed to be an actual collision. Here was no smell. There was smell, so strong, so evil, we seemed to have to push through it. When we broke out of it on the other side, vestiges followed us, clinging to our skins, our clothes. It neither shook off, nor brushed off.

Out of Bellingen on the North Coast of New South Wales, the sweetish, nauseating stench of a piggery flows like a fetid river down a long, green, beautiful valley.

By the carelessness of a neighbour a couple of hundred of our sheep once contracted footrot. That disease is as it sounds. Bacteria invade the hoof. The tissues go rotten. The horn lifts from the coronary cushion, green flies crawl in and lay their eggs. Sheep carry the sore hooves. When both front legs are affected the sheep goes down on its knees and crawls about the paddock. When our sheep were affected, the only cure was to cut off all the diseased tissue with clippers made for the job and steep the foot in a solution of bluestone or formalin. There are kinder and surer cures now.

Hour after hour I pared away rotten hoof and flesh. Blood spurted out of the trimmed hooves, reddened the trough of formalin. Maggots crawled about my boots. The floor was slippery with blood and squashed maggots. The hideous pile of clippings rose beside me, to be shovelled away and burnt when the job was done. All I became aware of was the pervading stench of footrot and the cadaverous smell of formalin.

Must from the old Municipal Library in Market Street, Sydney, sprawled out on to the footpath. I pushed through

Celebration

it as a youth up the wide, dull-grey staircase; I floundered through it at the shelves. The grey-faced librarians dressed in funereal brown. The place might have been a tomb of dead books. But the books came to life in my hands. Handling them resurrected them. The library – it is closed now – had big volumes of folk songs complete with music. I have never seen the books anywhere else. Most countries of the world had their own volumes. And some of the songs were bright enough to set the whole, sedate place dancing:

> Frau Kratzefuss, Frau Kratzefuss
> Giebt allen einen abschiedskuss.
> Fidi-ra-la-la. Fidi-ra-la-la.
> Fidi-ra-la-la-la-lah.

The Teachers' Federation library in Phillip Street that I attended by grace of an aunt smelt of new books as well as old. It smelt cleaner. It smelt of knowledge. I learnt a great deal about human sexuality from a tome on *The Sex Life of the Greater Apes*. On the shelves, as though they were ordinary books, were rare early-nineteenth-century copies of the books of Aphra Behn – *Oroonoko,* I remember, and many of her plays. The first of English women novelists, she lived in the eighteenth century before the hypocritical Victorians subdued women. An English barber's daughter, she grew up in Surinam in South America before the Dutch took it over. She spoke Dutch fluently, and King Charles II sent her to the Netherlands as a spy during one of the many Dutch wars. Dutch admirals and sea captains, presumably her bed mates, spoke freely to her, and she brought back accurate information about the moves and projected moves of Dutch shipping which the king's foolish admirals ignored, at great cost to English shipping. So she renounced politics for writing factual stories and popular, bawdy plays.

There were other old books by better writers in the library. I do not know why she interested me so much. Probably because the books were beautifully produced on heavy paper with old-fashioned lettering. As well, she was a vital woman. I would pick up one of her books and she spoke to me across two hundred and fifty years. She made writing important.

That library, too, has gone. So has a second-hand bookshop in George Street. One walked through a narrow door, down narrow steps, into catacombs of books. There seemed no end to the space. Tables of books spread under the city. Everything smelt damp. I saw no other customers. The light was poor. But I could read in bad light then. I found a copy of *Ulysses*, newly published, newly banned. The proprietor sat at a table near the entrance, vague as his books, beside a yellow light. 'How much?' I asked. 'Five pounds' he said. Five shillings then was a fair unbanned price. I left the book there, hoping but doubting the world might some day grow sensible about books. Would James Joyce have written the gibberish of *Finnegans Wake* if the world had not condemned him? How does a writer cope sanely with a wealthy wowser buying the whole first edition of *Dubliners* and burning it publicly in Dublin? As far as Joyce was concerned he burnt Dublin.

In Australian forests one can drive through scented tunnels, through great seas of perfume. Wattles smell yellow. The rich, sharp, sweet perfume could be no other colour. In a good spring in the great Pilliga forests, Mudgee Wattle blooms in thousand-hectare masses. Branches sag to the ground with the weight of balls of blossom. The air smells happy. On some tracks tall Motherumbah touches branches across the top. Fuzzy spikes of flowers wall the road, roof it, carpet it. Dropped blossom mirrors what is above it. For a kilometre or more one drives through scented yellow light.

The pale-flowered acacias, Hickory and Mountain Hickory with small white or lemon balls of flowers are more delicately scented. The perfume fades with the colour. They mass in the foothills of the Warrumbungles and in their season flavour fifteen kilometres of our road to town.

The singular grass trees give less public performances. They live their long, slow lives on poor soils in undisturbed places. Blackboys is their popular name. And so they look from a distance with black trunks and bulging grass skirts. One comes on big companies of them standing singly or in

Celebration

clumps over several hundred hectares. Always, at first sight, they look startlingly human. They add one ring of long green leaves a year a head-length below the top of the trunk. When they are about two hundred years old they stand one and three-quarter metres tall. They are human height with a head-sized top, and a green cape falling over a bulky brown skirt. The new leaves hang down over the dead and dying layers of past years. Often they trail on the ground. Some New Guinea women do not discard a tattered grass skirt. They add another over the top, and keep on adding until the bulk becomes uncomfortable. Then they strip them all off and begin again.

Fire renews the grass trees. They look so susceptible to fire, as though the burning leaves would consume the trunk and leave nothing there. But the unburnt long-skirted grass trees flower only at long intervals, perhaps after fifty years or so. Fire teases them into flowering.

They look dead after fire, just spongy black columns coated with soot. In two or three months the new bright green skirts grow about sixty centimetres long. Then, after the first good rain, the whole company of grass trees send up flowers at once, thick creamy spikes a metre and more long straight up out of the top of the trunks. They glisten with nectar. Native bees, honey bees, wasps, butterflies and moths swarm about them. A pungent scent washes about everywhere, warm, titillating, much like that of semen.

The low-growing iron grasses are relations of the grass trees. They produce little white cylinders of flowers with a scent so sweet and pervasive one sometimes finds the scent but not the flower.

Sundews produce imitation nectar on the ends of tactile hairs. They grow as hairy pink rosettes that colour hundreds of hectares of damp ground, or as taller plants with hairy, tentacle-like shoots on the seeping banks of creeks. Humans cannot smell the extraordinarily sticky droplets at the ends of the hairs. To insects it promises exquisite feasts. They ignore their favourite flowers to sup at the new nectar. One drop can snare an insect as powerful as a honey bee. It buzzes, vibrates its wings. The plant shows no feeling. It receives its victims impassively. It reacts so slowly it shows no movement. But during many hours the hair bends downward into the leaf carrying the struggling insect with it. Nearby hairs bend over imperceptibly. After fifteen hours one hair dabs its blob on the bee, helps with the pushing, after twenty hours another. Finally seven or eight hairs bend over the bee forcing it down on to the leaf. Then each hair in contact reverses its role. Instead of exuding fluid it sucks it back. The liquid is a digestive agent as well as a glue. The hairs drain the bee leaving only the shell. As they straighten they lever the body over the side of the leaf – it might take a fortnight. Then they exude false nectar again and wait for the next victim. Flies, mosquitoes, butterflies, moths, ants, spiders, beetles, bugs, representatives of most creatures that fly and crawl, feed the hungry plants. They take more than they need, a hundred where one would do. They fear poverty like misers.

I sit to write on a chair of leather and Australian rosewood made by a craftsman. The rosy grain is good to look at, the texture delicate to feel. Apart from the obvious senses one sits among a soft perfume, a suggestion of distant roses. Offcuts of the timber have been used in perfume making instead of attar of roses.

Cypress pine flooring enriches a house. Delicate incense rises from the floor. It rises from cypress cladding, too, but usually pine walls are painted. Odour and colour are fossilised in acrylic plastic. I do not like the smell of paint. I do not like the harsh colours.

Burning Dogwood is as fetid as a company of farts. Bushmen have spoilt meals by an unrecognised log of it on the camp fire. We season our winter fires with several timbers. The basis of the fire is box or ironbark. Pine smells good burning but it burns too fast and spits dangerously. It showers red-hot coals a centimetre in diameter four or five metres. Box and ironbark burn hot, burn moderately, and with little ash. Roots and knots vary the flames. They swirl around them, leap, burn calmly, change colour as they encounter different densities of wood. Pockets of gas generate and burst out, hissing needles of flame. Hollow logs suck flames in one end and spurt them out the other. A forked log forks the flames. They issue in different colours at different speeds. And when the log with the hollow,

Celebration

consumed outside and in to a shell, collapses into a mound of light red coals, fuzzy flames move over them like glowing moss.

Occasionally we put on a log of myall or budda, a root of oak. A gentle incense surrounds the room, adds fragrance to the lingering tang of the dry eucalypt leaves we always throw into the kindling. The room holds the fragrance all summer through. It could belong to no other country.

Gum Leaves Burning

Twisted roots of box, a hollow ironbark knot
Burn in pastel oranges and blues, brown, green,
   mauve and black.
The chimney draws as chimneys ought.

Nervous flames record each light
The wood grew by. A spectrum of two hundred years
Warms us this one winter's night.

The smell hangs lightly in the room
Of handfuls of dried gum leaves thrown among the
   kindling:
A certain testimony to an Australian home.

Those leaves give permanence to flame.
As mountains crumbled, as parades of people
   withered by the hearth,
First fire, last fire, they smelt the same.

We get out of bed unhurriedly. After the joyful waking we need time to absorb the promise of the new day. Haste spoils it. It takes the day for granted. Our time is not static. No seasons repeat themselves. At length lifted sheets release the smell of semen and the several female juices no one has named. The two smells are distinct but complementary. I make the fire in the closed box of the slow-combustion stove. It crackles out the sharp smell of pine chips. I cut bread thickly and toast it in a pre-heated toaster that takes thick slices. It smells crisp. Steam from the teapot promises the flavour of broad-leaved Darjeeling tea. Outside dew drips from the grass to ground and catalyses the deep odours of soil. Open the windows a little wider. The early day sounds rich and smells rich. It will finally absorb all the senses.

Free Choice

Postscript in memory of Joan

It amazes me that in the history of literature no other writer has estimated his senses. One would expect this book to be four hundred years old, or a rumour of something on clay tablets stored in a cave three thousand years ago. Perhaps the difficulty of writing it deterred them. I sat down each morning to dozens of fresh slips of paper with scribbled lists of what seemed intractable and unconnectable experiences. For hours my imagination had to relive them, then link them. As patterns formed I numbered the slips so I would not forget, then began to write. Perhaps the courage needed for such a work deterred them. A good writer always risks himself, but this was written with bared nerves.

Medieval artists represented the senses simply in various forms. In the Cluny Museum in Paris, one of the world's greatest tapestries, woven about 1490, depicts the senses through a girl, a unicorn, and other animals in a formal garden. In the first scene she holds up an ornate mirror for the unicorn to admire himself, in the second she plays a portable organ while one of her maids pumps the bellows, in the third she takes a sweetmeat from a bowl – her parakeet and a monkey are already eating, in the fourth she makes a nosegay of carnations while the monkey squats beside her basket smelling a flower he has filched from it, and a kid lies in the garden with its nose to a growing flower. In the fifth scene the girl strokes the spiral horn of the unicorn. But then there is a sixth scene to satisfy the uneasy philosophers of the day, the Free Choice. The girl has removed the intricate necklace she wore in the other scenes and is putting it in a cushioned box held up by the maid. Behind her is an empty bell-shaped tent that will shut out the world when she enters it. Philosophers believed that a man's mind developed only when he overcame the passions,

Free Choice

the submission to the senses. That was the free choice: to luxuriate in passion, or to subdue it and nurture the intellect. The idea still holds among some people. It is a theory that denies life.

An animal is its senses. They are its assessment of life, its total capacity. Man is animal. Our intelligence is a distillation of the senses, an appraiser certainly, but never an impartial judge. Even in those regions where the intelligence seems to function independently, in pure mathematics for example, I suspect there are roots within the senses.

Only two years after finishing this book I could no longer write it. I had no thought of the first edition as a completion. I was living what I wrote. The good times were past. The best times seemed to be coming. Joan died of cancer thirty years too young on 29 January 1985. The colour of our world changed.

I introduced Joan at a time of crisis – giving birth. Now meet her dying. She had eaten nothing whatever for over a fortnight, she could not turn in bed, she could barely talk. Kerry and I had washed her where we could reach, we had stroked her with oil. Now we needed to turn her. She lay naked between us, so pale and so strangely thin we discussed with unusual seriousness how best to move her. Kerry had become an experienced and excellent physiotherapist. 'We have to bend her sore knee ' she said, 'we can bend it to there if we do it very gently, and the other knee up to there.'

'I'll put a hand under her hips and lift while you push.'

'Yes, and I'll lift her head a little at the same time. We've got to be so careful with her head. Oh, that shoulder! Pull it forward a little or it will roll too far under her.'

We felt Joan shaking and looked quickly to see what was wrong. She was laughing. Joan never lost the capacity to amaze me. She enlivened all my senses.

Making love to her after thirty years was as profound an experience as our first adventures. Memories unconsciously deepened it, I suppose. The three remarkable children we had produced confirmed what we did, so did the certainty that knowing one another revalued the world for each of us.

One night when Joan was on top, riding me as nimbly as she

Celebration

had always done, I was startled to notice the light glinting on a few grey hairs.

'What are you looking at?'

'Your face. It's a lovely face to watch. It's setting in concentration. And now your eyes are growing dark.'

Do a woman's eyes darken as she nears orgasm? I always meant to watch closely to see how Joan's eyes did change. But that intent always got lost in passion.

Her nipples lost their colour months before she felt unwell. She cried. 'They're virgin pink again ' I said, 'and look! They still stand up as well as ever.'

'I don't like them any more ' she said, 'they don't look like me.'

We married in 1954. Joan was a pharmacist who intended to remain a pharmacist to keep her own identity. That was unusual thinking for those days. And she seldom wore dresses or skirts. They shortened her stride. Trousers and riding boots suited her. She used little make-up, perfume never. Very occasionally she would put on one of the necklaces I bought for her. She was so superbly woman she needed no wiles, no props to verify it.

Her voice identified her – quiet with a lively resonance, her smile, her laugh. She had such joy in life it seems absurd to have snatched it from her so young. Eating with her was a delight. She would sit down to a meal she had cooked, take an enthusiastic sip of wine, say 'Lord! We live well, don't we?' In a restaurant we never sat dumbly like some long-married couples. We swapped spoonfuls, forkfuls. Joan had such remarkable smell and taste she could usually list the ingredients of each sauce. She criticised. She mopped up her plates. She enjoyed hugely.

In her last week she could not even drink water, but she could suck ice. So she demanded two complete cubes at a time, one for each cheek. She took all she could fit in of her last contact with life.

At first she was angry with her disease. She had never spent a day in bed, she still looked exuberantly healthy. She could not believe she was mortally sick. It offended a deep belief that sickness was mostly an attitude of mind. I found her under the shower slapping herself with the soap, crying with frustration. 'What's the use of washing my outside when I'm all rotten inside? My immune system won't listen to me, it's out of control. I say to myself over and over, "Get well! Get well! There's so much to do " but nothing happens.'

Her anger was a wonder, her entire body expressed it. A couple of weeks after she died I had to leave the house unattended for a few days so I handed in her bank cards. It seemed safer, but it seemed also brutally soon to destroy something so completely hers. Irrationally I knew her anger if she came back: I could see her, hear her, stamping along the verandah, chin jutted forward, voice deeper, eyes seemingly projecting her fury. 'You never gave me a chance to come back. I'd only been dead a fortnight and you cancelled my credit cards. Now I'll have to apply for new ones. I'll never buy anything with them for you as long as I live!'

It is Joan happy that are the firmest memories, her laughter, her lilting 'Hullo!' on the telephone, her cry when she came back from a few days away at work, or a few weeks, 'I've brought you a present!' I would hear the car pull up, go straight out to meet her. She would be reaching for her heavy pharmacy books on the front floor, or round to the back seat for a carton of little bottles to be washed, or groceries. She would hand me a parcel. 'I've brought you a present,' she would say as she kissed me. It might be an out-of-print book I had been looking for, the first Spanner Crabs the travelling fisherman brought inland, a few luxuriously expensive European chocolates, but usually something very simple made valuable by the way she gave it.

'I love you, my darling' I told her again a few days before she died. I had to strain to hear her response. 'I love you, my darling' she said in return, then, more clearly, 'It's strange. I can't remember any more all the wonderful things we've done together, only that they were wonderful.'

I was kissing her when she could no longer talk, her forehead, her eyes, down the cheeks cold with ice. When I reached her lips I realised she was trying to kiss me back, so hungrily yet so lightly I could barely feel it. Those whispered kisses stay with me more than any others. It was the last time she kissed me.

'I want to crawl right inside you and stay there' she would

Celebration

say as she clutched me in those hours of night when the prospect of death seemed grimmest. 'You had, Joan, you had!' And I was no protection whatever.

Joan especially loved the first pungent flare from the eucalyptus leaves we put on the fire. She gathered them even at night if we had not set the fire early. When she died there was an extraordinary January flowering of Blue-leaved Ironbark on forest ridges forty kilometres away. So all the family drove out to cut branches of the fuzzy cream flowers and long leaves. Despite dry weather there were yellow paper daisies in bloom and masses of a tall white everlasting with tiny double flowers clustered into showy heads. We picked them, too, also dwarf casuarina heavy with cones, and a little plant, Pomax umbellata, that had finished flowering and dried off, leaving circles of empty cinnamon-coloured cups standing up like two-centimetre umbrellas.

We came home and cut sheaves of oat grass on our own farm. My sister made them all up into beautiful big bunches that we piled over Joan's coffin in the crematorium. Nicola and Philippa, our two granddaughters, carried little bunches of the lavender that Joan grew to remind her of her English ancestors. They were tied together with perfect white bows. I held Philippa up to place hers on. As I leant her forward she threw it impulsively and it landed upside-down on Joan's name-plate. I did not straighten it. I thought I heard Joan laughing.

That gladdened me; the rest of the day brightened. Even in death she could restore me. We could always do that for each other. 'There must be thunderstorms about somewhere,' she would say, 'the air's heavy. I feel depressed. Give me a kiss!'; or sometimes when she had driven home one hundred and fifty kilometres after a day's work, 'I'm a bit tired tonight. Give me a kiss!' When I ran out of words at my desk, when the room seemed lonely, I would get up, find her, perhaps say nothing at all, just kiss her, cup a breast or a buttock in a hand, then go back to work restored by the reality of flesh.

Joan had no funeral service, she wanted none. 'I don't believe in afterlife' she said. 'I'm here now, poof! I'm gone.' I am not so sure, though I have no belief in conventional

Free Choice

religions. No just God would permit so many millions to worship so fervently such diverse gods if He ordained only one True Faith. The world, the universe, the universes cannot be merely a game for some Supreme Intelligence, or worse a convent designed for His adoration. The more one learns, the more it seems that some master intelligence does organise it all, though not to the extent of overseeing individuals. Perhaps the complexity of time accounts for everlasting life: what is, what was, what will be, somewhere or everywhere, have happened, will happen, or are now happening. What I feel sure of is that some day I will know. I do not believe that a supreme intelligence would move so many lesser intelligences about on such a bewilderingly complicated board without ever allowing them to read the rules. That would reduce infinity to nothing.

Whatever her belief, Joan's spirit will live in this book. I need reality. Gratitude for having known her is sustenance, but I have never looked backwards for experience. I look ahead. What is ahead?

Among over two hundred letters in memory of Joan, one from Nancy Keesing said 'The Jewish phrase to a mourner is "I wish you long life" because it is believed that *how* people live; what they contribute to their families and friends and their community is all-important and what they should be celebrated and remembered for. Mourners should mourn – but also live.

'Eric – I wish you long life.'

I no longer measure time in years, I reckon it in books. I wish myself four more good books.

Baradine
April 1985

Acknowledgements

Of the five poems in this book, 'Water Rat' was first published in the *Sydney Morning Herald*, 'Meg Going to Bed' in *Overland*, 'Deciduous' in *Poetry Magazine*, 'Dinner' in the *Bulletin*, and in *Sheaf Tosser*, Angus and Robertson, 1967.